5 STEPS TO AUTHOR SUCCESS

WRITE BOOKS READERS LOVE AND BECOME A FULL-TIME WRITER

RACHEL MCLEAN

ACKROYD PUBLISHING

CONTENTS

Foreword   v

1. What to Expect From This Book   1
2. Why 5 Steps?   4

PART I
STEP ONE - MINDSET

1. Why Mindset Comes First   13
2. The Successful Author Mindset   15
3. Put Readers First   20
4. Surround Yourself with the Right People   23
5. The Myth of Writer's Block   27
6. Distancing Yourself From Your Book   33
7. Don't Quit   36
8. Making the Shift from Amateur to Pro   40
9. Mindset Resources   44

PART II
STEP TWO - RESEARCH

10. Why Research?   47
11. Researching Genre Tropes   49
12. Researching the Market   56
13. Researching Story and Craft   62
14. Research Resources   66

PART III
STEP THREE - CRAFT

15. The Importance of Craft   69
16. The Venn Diagram of Craft   71
17. Improving Your Craft   77
18. How to Write a Page Turner   83
19. Craft Resources   89

PART IV
STEP FOUR - LAUNCH

20. What I Mean by Launch	93
21. Stop! Don't Put Your Book Out There Till It's Ready	95
22. Routes to Market	97
23. Getting your Book in the Best Possible Shape	113
24. Strategically Seeding Book Sales	120
25. Adapting for Future Releases	134
26. Launch Resources	137

PART V
STEP FIVE - LONGEVITY

27. The Two Faces of a Sustainable Author Career	141
28. Build An Army of Fans	143
29. WIBBOW and Knowing Your Priorities	148
30. When to Get Help	151
31. Owning Your Work	154
32. Adapting to change	157
33. Loving what you do and avoiding burnout	162
34. Longevity Resources	165
Becoming a bestseller	166
Acknowledgments	171

FOREWORD

Many of us dream of making a living from writing. I know I did.

Ever since I was nine or ten years old, concocting stories in English lessons, I've longed to spend my time making up stories for a living. And now I'm lucky enough to do it.

I've been writing seriously for about seventeen years. I wrote the first draft of my first novel when I was pregnant with my eldest son. I had high hopes of using my maternity leave to get it published.

Little did I realise just how much work was involved in looking after a baby.

The book went into a drawer and didn't come out again until I joined a writer's group some years later. That book became the Division Bell trilogy. It's a set of books I'm proud of and which got great reviews.

But it didn't sell well.

It certainly didn't sell enough for me to give up my day job as a freelance technical writer and become a full-time novelist.

Foreword

And so in early 2020 (yes, just months before the pandemic hit), I sat down and took a good long, hard look at my writing career.

I knew that although I was lucky enough to be making a living writing nonfiction, it wasn't what I loved doing.

What I really wanted to do was write novels, reach more readers and give up my day job. And I'm pretty sure that's the goal of at least 50% of writers. It's certainly the goal of plenty of the writers I know.

So, I took a couple of months off writing. I spent that time working out a plan. That plan set out in detail precisely how I would switch from being a writer who got great reviews, but not such great sales, to one who sold by the bucketload.

My two crime series (Detective Zoe Finch and Dorset Crime) have now sold almost half a million copies between them. And that's in less than two years.

I started with no platform and a budget of around five hundred pounds. At the time of writing, I've got five books in the Amazon UK Kindle top 100. I sell thousands of books every day.

I'm not only making a living; I'm making an excellent living. And I'm secure in the knowledge that I'm building up security for my future and that of my children.

But wait… I know what you're thinking.

You've never heard of me.

That's because I'm an indie. I'm entirely self-published in fiction, so I don't get the kind of PR a traditionally published author gets. But I still find enough readers to maintain a successful career and sell thousands of books each day. And in October 2021 I won the Kindle Storyteller Award, so my books must be doing something right.

I'm extremely happy about where I've got to in the last

Foreword

two years. But don't get me wrong. As a full-time writer, you'll still worry about waking up one morning and discovering that the bottom has fallen out of your readership. You'll have great months where you pinch yourself and wonder if it will continue. And that's why maintaining your career and your readership is a very important part of this book – this is no get rich quick scheme.

My goal in this book is to help you come up with your own plan. It won't be the same as my plan, because your circumstances will be different from mine. And so will your writing.

But I hope to inspire you with my own example, to help you identify what you can do differently and how you can reach more readers, sell more books and make a living from your writing.

I'm not ashamed of wanting to sell books and make money from my work. After all, I've got bills to pay and food to put on the table. And if I didn't make money from my books, I'd have to find another job. That job would take me away from writing and would be nowhere near as much fun.

Don't be ashamed of wanting to make money from your books. You can write wonderful books you're proud of, and still make very good money from them.

If this is something you want to do – and if you've picked up this book and got this far, my guess is that it is – read on and find out how I went about changing the trajectory of my writing career, and how you ca

Rachel McLean, December 2021

1
WHAT TO EXPECT FROM THIS BOOK

This book isn't going to give you a formula for writing and marketing a bestselling book.

It's not going to tell you exactly how to structure your book so that readers will find it satisfying (although it will help you work that out).

Neither is it going to give you specifics on exactly how to use advertising or other marketing techniques to push your book into more people's hands (but it will tell you what I did that worked).

Instead, this book is going to help you take a step back from your writing and your marketing efforts, and identify the approach that will help you become a bestseller.

My goal is to help you think strategically, not tactically. I don't want to update this book every time an ad platform changes, or KDP make alterations to their publishing platform. Instead, I plan for this book to be evergreen.

That's why in the first section, I'll be talking about mindset.

I know a lot of authors, both traditionally published and indie (as well as hybrid). In the main, what differentiates the successful authors from those who are still trying to get published, or sell more books, is mindset.

I'm not talking about a specific technique you use to write books or to market them. Instead, it's a way of thinking about your craft, your books and your career.

Before you write a single word, or fire up an ads platform, I want you to start by considering how you think about your writing. I'll share with you the changes in mindset that I adopted before I became a successful author. Of course, I can't guarantee that what I did will work for you – which is why I won't be tactical and specific. If I were to tell you exactly how to use Facebook ads and Amazon ads to launch your books, that would be ridiculous. Your books are different from mine. Your audience is different from mine. Your experience of advertising platforms and your budget are different from mine. So you can't just copy what I did.

But what I hope to show you is that by thinking a certain way and adopting certain approaches towards the writing and the selling of your books, you can identify the log jams in your writing career.

I'm not going to give you a formula or a checklist, because there isn't one.

Instead, I'll give you tips and anecdotes from my own experience and that of other authors. Hopefully, these will help *you* see what it is *you* need to do.

You're going to have to do the hard work. Sorry.

But I hope to help you ensure that the hard work you do is the right kind of hard work. Not the kind of work that sends you round in circles and gets you nowhere.

Have I put you off? Were you looking for me to tell you exactly what to do?

No? Excellent. Keep reading.

2

WHY 5 STEPS?

The five steps in this book are the mindshifts or activities that helped me become a more successful author.

Five is a nice round number. It's not too big to be unwieldy, or so small that there's nothing to get your teeth into.

Let's have a quick look at what the five steps are.

Step 1 - Mindset

The first step is mindset.

This is where I'll tell you to stand back.

You work on this step away from your computer, without writing a single word or spending any money.

You don't even need to be on social media to do it (hurray!).

Mindset is all about the way you *think* about your books, your writing, and your author business. The three of those will be all tangled up with each other in a way that will change over time.

But if you're going to be a successful author, whether that's indie like me, traditionally published like a lot of authors, or hybrid, the first thing I think you should look at is your mindset.

And in the first part of the book, I'll help you identify aspects of mindset that might help you write more successful books and better manage your author career.

Step 2 - Research

The second step is research.

Any successful author worth their salt will be constantly learning and seeking out information and knowledge.

Authors who want to have people clamouring for their next book will be improving their craft, developing their stories, and writing better and better books over time. This means learning from craft books and from lots and lots of reading. Yes, every moment you spend reading is research. It helps you understand what works in terms of writing and story.

But it's not only craft and writing you need to research. You also need to understand your genre, and the marketplace where your books will sit.

If you're submitting to agents, they will want you to be able to say where your book fits. What genre is it, and who are your comps: in other words, whose books does it compare to?

If you're indie, knowing this is essential to being able to effectively market your books to people who are likely to buy them, love them, and become fans for life.

So, ideally before you write the first draft, it pays to

develop a deep understanding of your genre. What is it that people love about the most successful books? What are the tropes? What can you get away with subverting? And which books do you love reading?

As well as that, you'll need to learn about business and marketing. Yes, even the traditionally published authors, as your publisher will expect you to do most of the marketing. In fact, I'd argue that if you're going into business with a publisher, you need to do even more research, as you need to understand precisely what you're getting into before you sign. And once you do sign, there's no going back.

Learning about business and marketing – it sounds dull to some of us (not to me). But it's part of mindset. If you aren't prepared to learn all the aspects of the author business, you're unlikely to be a bestseller.

Step 3 – Craft

No book on becoming a successful author would be complete without significant mention of the craft of writing.

I'm deliberately calling it craft here, and not art, and that's because I believe that if you see yourself as a craftsperson, you're more likely to find a large audience.

Yes, writing as art has its place. But do those books sell enough to pay your mortgage?

Craft versus art is something I argue about with my writer friends all the time.

I don't think of myself as an artist. It makes me shudder to use what I think of as pretentious language to describe myself. (This is me – if you think of your writing as art, then that's great, although it won't make any difference to your sales.)

Instead I think of myself as a craftsperson. Writing great

stories that people love is something that can be learned, which is what makes it craft. It's not something that will come to you in a blinding flash of light.

Don't wait for it. Go out there and grab it.

The best way to develop your craft is to flex that muscle. In this book, I'll help you identify systems and techniques you can use to be more productive, to keep improving, and to write words and stories that readers love.

Step 4 - Launch

The fourth section is where we finally come to marketing.

Now, if you're traditionally published (or you want to be), you might be thinking this section isn't for you. But I would urge you to read it, partly because it will help you understand the language that your publisher talks. And partly because very few traditionally published authors aren't expected to do at least some of the marketing themselves.

I'll also include submitting to agents or publishers as part of your launch plan, as many of the same principles apply. But I can't deny that most of this section will be aimed at indies.

In this section, I'll help you identify the best time to start marketing your books and your author brand. This might mean launching a book or a series, or it might mean relaunching.

There are gazillions of tips and nuggets of advice bandied around the internet on this topic. And I don't necessarily agree with all of them. But as with everything in this book, don't take my word for it. It might – it probably will – work differently for you. I'll tell you what worked for me, and I'll outline why I did it that way – instead of telling you to copy me.

Step 5 - Maintenance

The fifth and final section of the book is possibly the most important.

It's relatively easy to have one book that's a success, particularly if you're traditionally published. It's an all-too-common story: the writers who have one breakout book and then find themselves sinking into mid-list obscurity.

But if you want to maintain an author career for the rest of your life, you'll need to consider how you'll work in the long term.

That will mean reader engagement and building an army of fans. It'll mean forging relationships with professionals and with other authors. No one can run an author business alone, and I doubt anyone would want to.

It's also about deciding what kind of writer you want to be. How many books will you write each year? Will you write in series or standalone? Will you stick to the same genre, or the same pen name?

These decisions won't just be informed by business benefits – you also need to consider what you enjoy and what will keep you motivated. There's no point in giving up your day job to become a writer, if you end up hating the writing.

I'll help you devise systems that will help make long-term productivity easier. I'll help you work out if you'd rather take the pressure off your writing with a day job. And I'll help you see how, by being flexible, you can stay in this for the long haul.

* * *

THOSE ARE the five steps that will be covered in this book. As I've already said, I'll avoid being too specific. I'm not going to tell you exactly what I did to make my books successful. And I'm not going to tell you exactly what you should do.

Instead, I'll help you make sense of my experiences and those of other successful authors, and work out which elements of those could work for you, your writing and your author career. There is no one-size-fits-all answer, but there are things that will certainly make it easier.

In the next chapter, we're going to finally get started on step one: Mindset. See you there!

PART I
STEP ONE - MINDSET

1

WHY MINDSET COMES FIRST

Why did you start writing?

I started writing my first novel because I had a bunch of ideas clamouring to get out. I mind-mapped it in a few hours then rushed straight in to the first draft.

I never considered how I would find readers for it, or who those readers might be.

And I imagine most writers are the same – we have a book in us, and that's the most important thing. But if you want to be a successful writer, it pays to think about your potential readers too. And to think about – whisper it – marketing.

I know you want me to plunge straight into practical tips on how to write a book that's going to be a bestseller, and how to sell it to as many readers as possible.

But I don't believe it's possible to do any of that without the right mindset.

If you're an indie author, you need to develop a mindset

that will enable you to become your own publisher and marketing department and to run a successful business.

If you're traditionally published, you'll need the right attitude when it comes to working with publishers and agents - this will help you get a deal and make the most of it.

And having the right attitude towards your readers, including knowing what it is *they* want, will help any author regardless of how you're published.

So, before you start writing the book that's going to make you famous, or at the very least lets you quit your day job, it pays to consider your attitude towards your writing.

In this section, we'll look at what the successful author mindset is. I'll identity some of the differences between amateur writers and professional writers. I'll help you beat writer's block and see writing as your job. And I'll help you understand why you shouldn't quit – even if you can't get an agent or your books are barely selling.

Adopting the right mindset will make it easier for you to make rational, level-headed decisions about your writing, your business and your future. Decisions that don't rely on emotion or gut reaction, but are logical and taken with an eye to the long term.

Let's start by identifying what the successful author mindset looks like.

2

THE SUCCESSFUL AUTHOR MINDSET

I know a lot of writers. Almost every day I meet a new writer, either in the real world or online. To be honest, if I stopped accepting friend requests from other writers on Facebook, they'd probably close down my account for being Norma-no-mates.

But among the writers I know, there are people with very different attitudes and mindsets. And that's not a problem.

We all write for different reasons. I have friends who only write a few thousand words a year, and friends who are writing thousands of words every day. I have friends who've never published anything and don't intend to, and others who've published sixty novels in ten years.

Yes, some people are that prolific – and they're great writers, too.

When it comes to productivity and mindset, writers generally find themselves somewhere on a spectrum.

At one end is the hobby writer. Someone who writes the occasional story, or perhaps is writing a novel but isn't too worried about getting it published. They'll never write a bestseller – and that doesn't bother them in the slightest.

At the other end of the spectrum are the professional writers. They're producing a regular number of books every year and devoting time to writing and improving their craft. If they're self-published, they're selling enough books to make a living; if they have a book deal, they aren't worried about being dropped.

In between these two groups, you'll find the majority of writers. People for whom NaNoWriMo is a challenge but not an insurmountable one. People who sell, but not enough. People who take their writing and their careers seriously, most of the time, but not seriously enough or for enough of the working week to achieve what they really want to.

Chances are, if you're reading this, you're in the middle group. That's where I was two years ago. I wanted to be a professional author, but I was taking the wrong approach to my writing. When I shifted my mindset, everything changed.

To move into the second group, you need to change the way you think about your writing. You need, quite simply, to go from thinking like an amateur to thinking like a pro.

Ten characteristics of pro authors

Pro authors have a few characteristics in common:

1. They write regularly. If not every day, then at least twice a week.
2. They set writing targets and stick to them (most of the time).
3. They seek constructive criticism and act on it.
4. They put readers first.

5. When they finish writing their current work in progress, they move on to the next project.
6. They are able to look at their work dispassionately and understand that it's not a personal slight when someone doesn't like something they've written.
7. They want to get better at writing, publishing and selling books, and take active steps to do so.
8. They work with other professionals such as editors, proof readers, publishers and (if they're indie) book cover designers and marketing experts.
9. They network with other authors and actively seek out people they can learn from.
10. They're always trying new things: writing methods, story ideas, marketing techniques or publishing formats.

If there's one of these ten characteristics that in my view really marks out the pro, it's number 6. A professional author is able to separate themselves from their work. They can see that a bad review isn't a personal slight, and they're prepared to take feedback and use it to improve their work. In other words, they know that their work isn't just about them.

And if there's one characteristic that'll do the most to guarantee a bestseller, it's number 4: putting readers first.

Things you can do to shift to a pro mindset

Making the shift from an amateur to a pro mindset may seem daunting. If you've been stuck in a hobbyist rut for years, it's hard to see a way out, even if you're convinced that what you want, more than anything, is to write for a living.

This section of the book will help you see that way out.

Some of the things I did to shift my mindset, and that I've seen other successful authors do, include:

PUT READERS FIRST. Who are you writing for? Yourself, your family and friends, or your readers? If you're going to write a bestseller, you should be focused on readers.

SURROUND yourself with the right people. This sounds cynical, I know (especially if you're British like me). But if you want to be a bestseller and all your writer friends just want to write the occasional story, they won't be able to help you. Seek out people who inspire you and who you can learn from.

VIEW WRITING AS YOUR JOB. This means you will show up on a regular basis, and put the hours in. You can't write if you're not sitting in your chair ready to write. This also involves ridding yourself of the myth of writer's block - more of which later. (Note: you're unlikely to start making money from writing until you see writing as your job.)

GET feedback from reliable sources and act on it. Find people whose writing you admire, and get feedback from them. Get feedback from readers. And listen to what people say about successful books in your genre. Importantly, use that feedback to improve your writing and better meet reader expectations.

Move on to the next project. When you've finished your work in progress, move on to the next one. After all, you aren't someone who is writing *a* story or *a* book. You are *a writer*. Writers write more than one thing. This will help you build momentum, will create a larger catalogue for readers to find or publishers to accept, and will ensure that you keep improving through practice. It'll also help you detach your emotions from the last project.

ADOPT A LEARNING MINDSET. There's so much to learn about writing, publishing and marketing books. You can never know it all, and it's constantly changing. Actively seek to grow your knowledge and understanding, and keep abreast of the latest tools and trends.

PHEW! That's a lot to take in. Let's look at some of these in more detail, starting with readers. How do you put them first?

3
PUT READERS FIRST

Picture the scene. You're at a writers' group, introducing yourself to new people. You get chatting with a writer and you ask them what they're writing and who their book is for.

Their answer: 'everybody'.

This happened to me. I met a writer who told me their book was for everybody. I tried to get them to drill down, but they were insistent. Years, later, that book hasn't been published.

The reality is that if you target a book at everybody, *nobody* will think it's for them. You need to identify your readers, and focus on them.

The concept of putting readers first is at the heart of everything in this book. It's the most important thing you can do if you're going to write a bestseller.

After all, who is it that's going to buy, read and review your book and push it up the charts?

Readers.

Not your writer friends. Not your mum. Not your agent or your editor.

Readers.

They are the most important people in the publishing business. Followed by writers. Unfortunately, lots of people seem to have forgotten this.

So – how do you put readers first?

Firstly, you need to understand what people are reading and why. Banish any snobbery you have about the latest blockbuster and find out what made it such a hit. Yes, you hate Dan Brown's clunky prose, you're horrified by EL James's smutty content. Get over it.

These authors must be doing something right, or they wouldn't have found such success.

Ignore your writer friends, who probably have more highbrow taste than the average reader. Start reading books that sell in the millions. Especially if they're in your genre. Try to work out what it is about them that readers love.

Chances are it's got nothing to do with the quality of the prose. Instead, it'll probably be one of two things: a page-turning plot, or characters who the reader connects with. Even better: both.

If you can get one or both of these things right, readers will forgive pedestrian or even clunky prose. In fact, most readers prefer writing that doesn't draw attention to itself.

Spend time reading reviews by readers (not in the pages of the *New York Times* or the *Guardian*) and identify what they love about those books. That'll help you identify how to do the same thing.

. . .

As well as looking at those books, you can (whisper it) try making direct contact with readers in your genre.

Find the places they hang out, either online or in real life. That may be Facebook groups, online forums, conferences, or elsewhere.

What else do they love, beside those books? What TV shows do they watch? What movies do they rave about?

Watch those shows and movies and find out what they have in common with the popular books in your genre.

Engage with other readers. Not as an author (never, *ever* tell them to buy your book), but as another reader.

That way you'll get into their mindset. You'll start to understand what your potential readers want, instead of what your editor or your writing critique group wants.

And if you hate doing this? If you can't stand those movies or TV shows, or you don't enjoy reading the books in your genre?

There's an easy answer to that. Find another genre to write in. If you don't enjoy the writing, it'll show. And it'll make you miserable.

Move on, as quickly as you can. Find a genre you love. It'll make you so much happier. And you might surprise yourself. Don't get shoehorned into a genre you think you like and stay there regardless of how it treats you.

4

SURROUND YOURSELF WITH THE RIGHT PEOPLE

I've been writing since I was a kid. I wrote my first serialised story when I was about nine years old.

I haven't got a copy of it now, but my teacher loved it. I think that, more than anything, he was surprised by the idea of a nine-year-old writing a short novel.

I'm sure I'm not alone in this. I imagine there are people reading this thinking *yup, I'd written ten novels by the time I was five*, and that's great.

For most of my life, I wrote as a hobby. I wrote when the muse hit me, when I came up with an idea for a story. I loved it when I woke up in the morning with a story idea and couldn't wait to get down to my computer and bang it out on the keyboard.

But to become a professional writer, I had to become somebody who didn't just write when the muse was in the room. After all, and I know this is a cliché, but plumbers don't do plumbing when inspiration hits them.

. . .

It's VERY difficult to switch from being an *only when inspired* writer to an *every day even when it's raining* writer.

But a great way to kick yourself into gear is to surround yourself with people who show up and write.

I STARTED WRITING my first proper novel almost twenty years ago. I was commuting from Birmingham to Bristol, which was about an hour and a quarter on the train twice a week. Each time I would get on the train, same seat, same carriage, no decisions. Before the train had even pulled out of my station, my laptop would be open and I'd have started typing.

It became a habit. There were no distractions. No Wifi on trains in those days. No trolley coming along to sell me a cup of tea or a Twix. And so, on every day that I was commuting, I would type a chapter on the way there and a chapter on the way back.

That way, I wrote a book in six months. I was a writer!

But then, it all went pear-shaped. I thought I'd spend my maternity leave editing the book and getting it ready to send to an agent. But I seriously underestimated how much work is involved in caring for a baby.

I spent the next few years consumed by parenthood.

I briefly found a writers' group. I went along to a meeting, but shortly after that I discovered I was pregnant with my second son. I suffered from terrible morning sickness and fatigue, and stopped writing again.

It wasn't until some years later, when my oldest son was around ten years old, that I met someone who would change my writing life – at a coding club for kids.

One of the other mums was Heide Goody. She was a

published indie author, and the chair of a local writers' group.

She talked me into going along, and I got my mojo back.

It turned out that this was the same writer's group I'd gone to just once in the early months of my second pregnancy. But this time, I stuck with it.

I had no excuse. My kids were older. I could convince their dad to look after them when I was at meetings. And I became a regular attendee.

THAT GROUP CHANGED my writing life, for two reasons.

1. Attending a writers' group twice a month made me write between meetings. I wanted to submit work for critique, so I made sure I produced stories or chapters for submission.
2. I met people whose writing was better than mine, and who were writing more than I was. I watched them, sought their feedback, and learned from them. I still do.

IN THE YEARS since I met Heide, I've been a regular attendee. Out of the 160 meetings since I joined, I've attended 122 (yes, we keep those records!).

Going to that writers' group every fortnight ensured that I never forgot I was a writer. True, I might not have been getting paid to be a writer. I might not have admitted to strangers that I was a writer. But I was a writer... because I wrote.

. . .

But it wasn't just the writing that the group helped me with: it was mindset, too.

For example, Heide and her writing partner Iain Grant encouraged me to self-publish. Another member got a six-figure publishing deal, which inspired me. And the regular feedback I got on my writing motivated me to keep improving.

Through that group, I've met other writers who are regularly writing, regularly publishing. People who talk about books like a business, not a hobby.

If you can surround yourself with people like that, it will help you adopt that mindset. It will help you think professionally about your writing.

Take a look online. See if you can find a writing group in your area or online. Importantly, commit to showing up. That's the key thing: showing up to your work, and showing up to the people who inspire you to keep writing.

Over time, you'll meet yet more authors. They'll inspire you in different ways. Don't be scared to ask them questions and to learn from them. Even the biggest names were beginners once.

5

THE MYTH OF WRITER'S BLOCK

I'd be prepared to bet that there are people who hate the title of this chapter. Because writer's block affects us all, doesn't it? It can't be avoided.

I disagree.

Let's start by thinking about what it means to be a professional writer.

The Oxford English Dictionary defines 'profession' like this:

> 'any occupation by which a person regularly earns a living'

THAT MEANS IT'S A JOB. Not just the business side of it, like publishing, marketing, signing books etc. But the writing itself.

And if there's one thing you need to do for a job, it's to show up.

Even when you don't have any ideas, and you don't feel like it.

Writers and would-be writers love to talk about writer's block. People will lament the wasted hours, mournfully recalling how they had the best intentions, how they planned to sit down today and write 5000 words. But writer's block hit. For some reason, they couldn't think of anything decent to write.

And there's the rub.

It doesn't have to be good.

The important thing is to write. Even if your writing is dreadful, you can come back later and edit it. Even the best writing will need to be edited, so why not produce some dross and edit that instead?

It can be difficult talking yourself out of a belief in writer's block.

You sit down at your desk, feeling uninspired. You can't think up the next plotline in your story. So, you blame writer's block. You move away from your chair. You decide to spend some time faffing about on Facebook talking to people about your books, or maybe chatting to other writers about how hard it is being a writer.

None of that will help you write books or sell books. It won't help you get published and become a bestseller.

So, how do you beat writer's block?

Here are some of the things I've done over the years to help me write every day and get words down on the days when I'd rather poke my eye out with a toothpick.

Forget about quality

First drafts are sometimes referred to as vomit drafts.

Just get the story out there.

It doesn't matter how bad it is. You can come back and edit it.

Write the dross, and edit it later.

A few words is better than no words

Maybe you have a goal of writing a thousand words a day. Maybe you're doing NaNoWriMo and you need to write 1,667 words a day.

Today, you don't have much time. Not enough time for over a thousand words.

It doesn't matter. Just write as many words as you can. It'll exercise your writing muscle, and it'll edge you closer to your goal of finishing your WIP.

Don't try to catch up

Imagine yesterday was the day when you only managed 500 words. Today's goal is 1,667. Now you need to write 2,834 just to catch up, right?

Wrong.

If you do this, it'll only build up. If you only manage 1,000 words today, then you'll need to write 3,501 words the next day.

At this point, you'll give up. Writing over three and a half thousand words in a day will be too much to contemplate, and you'll be put off writing at all.

In no time, you'll be thousands of words behind.

Instead, forget how much you wrote yesterday. Hit

today's goal, today. And tomorrow. That way, on day three you'll only be 1,167 words behind, instead of 3,501. You can write a few extra words here and there over the next week or so, and catch up easily.

Or instead you can forget about catching up, and set yourself long-term deadlines that have a contingency built in. Maybe your intention is to write an 80,000 word manuscript, and you have 40 working days to do it. Don't tell yourself to write 2,000 words a day. Instead, set yourself a goal of 2,200 words each day. That way, if you get behind occasionally, you won't really be behind at all.

Set realistic goals in the long term, and tough goals in the short term. It's the opposite of what we instinctively do, but it's so much more effective. And every day you're supposed to write, write. Even if it's only 100 words.

Use tools to track goals and monitor progress

I use Excel spreadsheets every day. I note down how many chapters I've dictated (because that's how I write). You might track word count instead.

Set yourself a realistic target and track your progress against it every day. Doing this will help you see your progress. It'll give you a sense of pride when you meet your goals.

Make a public commitment

Tell other people when you're going to finish the first draft of your book.

If you're indie, hire an editor and tell them when it will be ready. Or agree to a deadline with your agent or editor if you've got a publishing deal (chances are you won't be able to avoid this).

Share your writing goals with writer friends – or with the whole world via social media.

This makes you accountable. You've got no excuses, so you're less likely to give up.

Don't assume that you need a keyboard to write

If you find it easier to write in another way, try it out.

For example, you might find that writing by hand makes it easier to for you to get the words down when you're out and about carrying a notebook. Or it might just feel more natural that way.

Or, like me, you might find that dictation means that you can 'write' more each day and in more flexible locations. I'm not the only one who finds that dictation helps banish the spectre of writer's block and keep me healthy.

Experiment with drafting and editing

A commonly repeated piece of advice is to write all of your first draft before editing any of it.

There are various theories about left vs right brain, creative vs logical brain. Most of them are pseudo-science.

If, in spite of everything, you are struggling with writer's block, try changing your routine.

I've experimented with different ways of mixing up writing and editing over the years. And what I find works best is to edit as I go. I dictate a few chapters, then edit them, then dictate some more. This way, I can make corrections as I go, and don't have to deal with the knock-on effects on an entire book if I make a mistake or a significant change to a plot or character.

Once I've got a batch of ten to twenty chapters ready, I'll send them to my editor. This means that he and I are working alongside each other, which makes the whole process faster as I don't have to wait for him to edit the entire book once it's done.

Try a few different methods: writing the whole first draft, putting it away, then coming back to edit after a gap. Editing as you go. Somewhere between the two. There isn't a one-size-fits-all answer.

Experiment with some different methods and find not only which works best for you, but which helps you motivate yourself to write.

* * *

I KNOW it's a controversial opinion, but I really believe that writer's block is something of a myth. No other profession talks about getting blocked. If something's your job, you turn up and do it. Whether you're in the mood or not.

And writing is just the same. I have plenty of days when I'd rather have a day reading than a day writing. But I show up. I hit my target and I make progress on my WIP.

That way, I'm constantly producing new words, new chapters, and new books to sell to readers.

If you can get past writer's block, it will exponentially increase your chances of becoming a full-time writer.

6
DISTANCING YOURSELF FROM YOUR BOOK

Your book is your baby.

You've sweated blood to write it.

You've risen at five o'clock in the morning, long before the rest of your family woke up, or you've worked till late at night while everybody else was sleeping. You found time between working hours or on your commute, and you gave up your social life.

However it is that you've managed to write your first manuscript, chances are it was hard work and it feels very personal. But if you want to be a bestseller, you need to distance yourself from your book once it's finished.

Why you should distance yourself from your book

One of the attributes you'll need if you want to be a professional author is resilience. And the more emotional you feel about your book or your books, the harder that is. You'll get feedback from professionals. It won't always be good. Sometimes it'll be terrible. Sometimes they'll be telling you to ditch this book and write another one. And that's before you get to the one-star reader reviews...

So, if you can try and think of your book as something separate from you, it'll help.

It's now a product. It's something you want people to buy. Those people might be agents or commissioning editors, or they might be readers. But whichever publishing method you're pursuing, it helps to think of your books dispassionately.

I know I suffered from this problem with my first book. I felt passionately about it. It touched on subjects that were important to me. It had taken me years to write. And so, when people left bad reviews, I took it personally.

But the reality is that they weren't leaving bad reviews for *me*. They were leaving bad reviews for that book. It was my first book: it wasn't my best work. And maybe it wasn't the book for them (I do wonder if some of those one-star reviewers ever read the blurb). But I can't do anything about that, and if I'd allowed it to dent my confidence, I'd never have written another word.

How to distance yourself from your book

My top tip for withdrawing emotionally from your book is to start writing the next one.

As soon as your current book is finished, put it aside. Send it out into the world, either by submitting it to agents or by putting it up for sale (after a professional edit). And then move on.

Start writing the next book. Then you'll become emotionally attached to that instead, and distance yourself from the last one.

By the time I get to publication day for each of my

books, I'm always at least halfway through the first draft of the next one. I often finish the next one at around the time the previous one comes out. It'll all depend on your publishing schedule.

Just write the next book. It'll help you be professional, and it'll give you another book to put out there and use to build your author career.

7

DON'T QUIT

We've all heard of them, haven't we?

Those overnight successes, who suddenly go from nothing to bestseller with their debut novel.

You watch people like that, and it's hard not to feel jealous.

But is anybody really an overnight success?

I bet if you talk to most people who suddenly achieved success, it wasn't sudden at all. It was probably after years of hard work. Those years might have been spent writing other novels that never saw publication, or writing novels that were published but didn't sell. Or hawking their manuscript around dozens of publishers.

If you're worried that you've been writing for five years, even ten, and you haven't seen success yet, it's still not time to give up.

When I nearly quit

I've been writing seriously for 18 years, but it wasn't until a year ago that I quit my day job.

Now, I didn't spend all of those years in between writing seriously, or chasing the goal of becoming a full-time author. Let's be honest: I was too busy raising kids and procrastinating. But I did start publishing in 2017. And like most people, I expected to see quick success. I was inspired by friends who were building an audience and selling books in good quantities.

I listened to podcast interviews with people who'd suddenly launched the most amazing ad campaign and found themselves selling thousands of books.

My first few books went down well with reviewers and readers. But then they fizzled out. After I'd written two trilogies, both very different (in itself not a wise move), two books in a series that flopped, and a standalone novel that I thought would make my name, I realised I was getting it all wrong.

I was seriously considering quitting.

Don't get me wrong, I love writing. And I would continue to write, even if it wasn't my job. But writing on a regular basis, setting myself deadlines, paying editors and other professionals to help in my business, those elements were starting to feel like a waste of time and money.

I was faced with a choice. Either I'd turn my writing career around, or I'd commit fully to my day job.

Urgh. My day job. It was better than many, but it was dull. And I was three years behind in terms of professional development – three years I'd spent learning about publishing.

If I was going to commit to the day job, I'd have to

catch up on those three years, something I really didn't fancy doing.

That's when I decided it was time for one last roll of the dice.

How I switched things up

I made a series of decisions that I determined to stick with.

I would switch genres and pick something with a huge audience (despite all the advice to find a niche).

I would research the genre and the tropes. I would look at what readers loved, and what other writers were doing that worked.

I wouldn't copy everything I saw, but I'd use it to inspire my own work.

There's no shame in watching what other people do, and cherry picking the bits that are appropriate for you. That's why you're reading this book. And businesses have done that since time immemorial.

It worked. I've now sold over 400,000 books in my first two crime series (across ten titles). I make a very good full-time living. And I love my job. So much more fun than my old freelance job!

Why not quitting was important

I believe that the reason that I achieved success from those crime novels so quickly wasn't just down to the research I did.

It was also because of the previous three years and the nine books I'd already written.

I'd spent those years learning how to publish and market

books. Writing nine books helped me develop my craft and learn how to tell a story readers enjoyed.

Without that experience, my first crime book, however well researched, wouldn't have been as good. I wouldn't have known how to publish it and my advertising efforts would have flopped.

All of which means that the time I spent persevering, learning the trade, learning how to write and market books (and how not to), was invaluable.

If you've spent the last five or even ten years slogging away at this, don't despair. That time wasn't wasted. You've learned how to write and you may well have been learning about publishing and marketing too.

You just need to bring it all together, with a professional mindset. You need to learn how to write for readers, and not for yourself. More on which in the next chapter...

8

MAKING THE SHIFT FROM AMATEUR TO PRO

Back in the days before I started writing crime, I had the idea of writing a kids' time travel adventure set in a Victorian school. I went to a place called the Black Country Museum where you can sit in the Victorian schoolroom and experience a lesson as it would have been in the nineteenth century.

The 'teacher' asked what had brought us there. I told him I was researching a book.

His response? "Ooh, get you."

It knocked my confidence. It made me feel like an idiot and an impostor. And it put me off telling strangers what I do for a while.

But that was wrong.

If you want to be a professional author, the biggest mindshift you'll need to make is to stop thinking of yourself as somebody who writes for a hobby – and start thinking of yourself as a writer.

I know it can feel pretentious when people ask you what you do and you tell them you're a writer. When that man mocked me, I wanted to either disappear into the floor, or punch him.

These days, it's easy to tell people I'm a writer, because I don't have another job. But there's no reason you can't tell people that you write, even if you do have a day job. It'll help you start to think of yourself as a professional writer.

SHIFTING from an amateur mindset to a professional one has implications outside just telling people you're a writer.

It means you commit to actually sitting down and writing. It means you think of your writing as something that could make you money in the long run. And it helps you think with a more businesslike frame of mind.

HAVING a professional mindset will influence every decision you make.

When you're deciding what to write next, you won't just think about what you feel like writing. You'll also think about your readers. What do they want to read? What are they clamouring for? Maybe you'll think about your agent or your publisher. What have they asked for next? What are they going to take on?

You'll also be thinking about how you'll market your next book, and where it fits in your genre. How does it complement your backlist, and will your readers want to buy it?

Thinking about these things is important if you're going to be successful. I'm not saying you shouldn't take into account what *you* want to write, too. That's important: if you don't enjoy writing, you might as well get a regular job.

· · ·

But books are products, just like anything else you buy, and you need to write and package a book that appeals to readers. One that makes people want to come back and read more.

So, the main shift from amateur to pro is taking your thoughts about your writing outside yourself. It's not just about what you want to write, but what other people will want to publish, buy or read.

For me, that changed in early 2020. I'd been writing and publishing my books for three years, and I'd seen a little bit of success, but not enough to earn a living. I'd written nine books in a range of related genres. They'd all got great reviews, but none of them sold more than a handful of copies a day. And sales were falling.

I hadn't done any research into my genre. I hadn't identified where they sat in the market, and I hadn't thought about what readers wanted. Instead, I'd just written the books I wanted to write.

Which was great, but not the best way to forge a career.

My day job at the time was freelance technical writing. It bored me senseless. I decided that writing any fiction, even if it didn't set me on fire, would be better than that. (It turns out the fiction I write now does set me on fire, which is a bonus.)

Writing to market had to be more fun than writing to order for clients.

In the end, writing to market has been a hell of a lot of fun. Because it's meant people reading my work and giving me feedback on it. It's meant that I've made readers happy, and come across people who talk about my characters as if they're real.

This morning I got a message from a reader with a disability, telling me my books had helped them get through some particularly dark days. If something like that isn't enough to make me want to get up and write in the morning, what would?

I love writing crime, which is the genre I picked when I decided to take things seriously. I love writing in series and being able to get my teeth into a longer story arc or a set of characters and explore them in greater detail. And I love the fact that my readers talk about *my* creations as if they were flesh-and-blood people.

There's nothing more satisfying than seeing people love your work. And by adopting a professional mindset, you can make that much more likely.

STOP WRITING FOR YOURSELF, and start writing for readers. It's as simple – and as hard – as that. In the next section of this book, on research, we'll look at how you can get into the heads of readers and identify what they love.

9
MINDSET RESOURCES

Here are some of the resources on mindset that have been helpful for me.

Books

- *The Indie Author Mindset* by Adam Croft
- *Lifelong Writing Habit* by Chris Fox
- *Let's Get Digital* by David Gaughran

PART II

STEP TWO - RESEARCH

10

WHY RESEARCH?

Writing and publishing is a business just like any other.

And in any other business, no one would launch a new venture without doing some research.

Research takes many different forms. It can be research and development for a new product. Market research. Or researching the skills required for the business.

Writing is a weird profession. Unlike other professions, there's a belief that writers are born and not made. That you can't learn how to become a better writer, but that somehow it has to happen as if by magic.

Even literary geniuses do their research. Take Shakespeare. His plays were almost all based on existing stories, so he must have researched those. He knew those stories were solid, and that they'd been entertaining people for a long time. And he was right there at The Globe, watching audience reactions to his plays and tweaking them as he went. Then there was Dickens: publishing what later became his books as serialisations, having access to reader feedback, and using it when writing the next instalment.

In this part of the book, I'll identify the kind of research I did to become a successful author, and which I imagine would benefit you.

When I started writing, I didn't do nearly enough research. I subscribed to the seductive idea that it should come instinctively.

I soon learned that wasn't the case.

When I spoke to people with more publishing experience than I had, I embarrassed myself through my lack of knowledge. I realised my own naivety when they answered my questions.

But there's nothing wrong with not knowing stuff - we all have to start somewhere. What *is* wrong is assuming that you can go on to become a successful author while *still* not knowing stuff, when it's all out there for you to learn. And yes, there will be exceptions: there are the lucky few who make it without all the hard work. But they're rare; that's what makes them notable, that's why you hear about them. For the most part, their strategies are no more valid as a guide to your own success than the blind luck of a lottery winner.

It didn't take me long to realise that my 'it all comes instinctively' attitude wasn't helping me at all. So, I embarked on strategic research. And in this section of the book, I'll show you the difference it made.

11

RESEARCHING GENRE TROPES

Understanding the genre within which you write is important, no matter which route to publication you want to take. Even if you haven't yet decided which route that will be.

Readers are very different from writers.

Writers tend to be magpies when it comes to our reading habits. We're more eclectic than the average reader and will flit between fiction and nonfiction, literary, genre, and anything in between.

We like to pick up nuggets of brilliance, no matter where it comes from. And we don't necessarily read exclusively in the genre we write in. Some genre writers don't read at all in the genre they write in, although that's not something I'd recommend.

All this means that as a writer, it's easy to get a distorted view of reader preferences and behaviour.

As somebody who's fascinated by books and literature, you'll probably pick up any kind of book, no matter what the genre or style. As long as it looks interesting.

You're less likely than the average reader to pick up a book because you think it looks like something you've read before. In fact, you might even be a bit snobbish about that idea. So derivative!

But the reality is, most readers (and particularly the readers who buy a lot of books) think very differently from us writers.

I write crime (mystery, if you're in the US). Specifically, I write UK-based police procedurals. That's a niche within the crime or mystery genre.

I decided to write crime when I realised my cross-genre, ideas-based books weren't selling enough to make a living. I enjoyed reading crime and I believed I'd be good at writing it. So I did lots of research. And I mean *lots*.

Understanding your genre

The first thing I had to understand were the subgenres within the crime and mystery genre. You'll need to do the same for your genre, but I'll share what I learned about mine by way of example.

The genre breaks down into two quite big headings: police procedural and cozy mystery.

Police procedurals will have professionals doing the detecting (normally police detectives, but sometimes crime scene investigators, pathologists, lawyers or other experts), and they tend to be darker in tone.

Cozy mysteries will feature amateurs solving crimes that they've come across in the course of their everyday lives. The tone will be lighter, with no gore, little reference to the :ath, and absolutely no bad language.

re also private investigator stories, which can of a procedural or a cozy. If you're writing a PI story, make sure you pick which side yours is on, and stick to it. In other words, are you writing VI Warshawski, or Hercule Poirot?

And within each of those genres, there are subgenres. Cosies have subgenres featuring animals, cooking, literature, or the paranormal. They might be rural or urban (but not gritty), and might feature a young (normally female) sleuth or an older one, male or female. They might be historical (many modern cosies are set when Agatha Christie was writing). Procedurals will have subgenres relating to the type of investigator (police or other, male or female), the amount of gore, and whether they focus on the perpetrator, or just on the investigators.

Within each of these genres and subgenres, there are tropes.

Firstly, for all of these books, there will be a crime. Normally a murder, but not always (it needs to be a serious crime though – I'll never write a book based on the theft of my campervan). The crime will be solved, and the solution will be (at least theoretically) achievable by the reader. Sherlock Holmes might have miraculously solved mysteries based on information unavailable to the reader, but that won't wash now.

Cozy mysteries will often feature a small town or a rural setting. The protagonist will be an amateur, sometimes armed with some specialist knowledge that helps them solve crimes. Or perhaps they're well connected in their community, or simply incredibly astute (like Miss Marple). They might have an old-fashioned feel (or they might not - but pick one of the two and stick to it).

Police procedurals will always have a professional whose job it is to solve the crime. Their motivation will be mainly professional. If it's also personal, that won't be related to the crime itself, but to something else going on in their life (e.g. the threat of being fired, memories of previous, unsolved crimes that have haunted them, etc.) They might have a team around them, in which case the reader will want to get to know them. And the book will be grittier than a cozy, with an urban setting more likely than not. If there's a rural setting, it'll be atmospheric rather than idyllic – think dark and brooding moors, not sunlit fields.

THIS SHORT BREAKDOWN is just scraping the surface of what I learned about crime and mystery. And as well as these thematic tropes, there are plot tropes.

THE CRIME WILL ALWAYS TAKE place towards the beginning of the book – sometimes it's happened before the book begins, and it's the discovery of the crime that kicks things off. There will be multiple suspects, and clues planted to make us suspect them all. There will be red herrings scattered among the genuine clues, but those will be explained at some point and won't be gratuitous. And, importantly, the case will always be solved. Readers of mystery like the sense of resolution and justice at the end of the book.

If you read a book with a crime in it that isn't solved, chances are that isn't a mystery: it's literary fiction that happens to feature a mystery. (The title often gives it away: it'll be long.)

THERE ARE ALSO TROPES when it comes to packaging and presenting the book. Cosies have very different titles and covers from procedurals. But I'll cover that in more detail in section 4 of this book.

Doesn't this make things boring?

I know what you're thinking.

If everyone who writes in a genre uses these conventions and tropes, then every book in that genre will be identical.

Of course not! Every book is unique, because of the specific way it's told.

You'll create different characters from those created by other writers, you'll have a different setting from those drawn by other writers, the nature of the crime (if it's mystery) will be different and also, of course, there's your unique author voice and style of writing.

To summarise: don't worry that by paying attention to genre tropes, you'll become derivative.

If you're a good writer, that won't happen.

THE SECOND REASON why it's important to ignore any writerly snobbery is because readers aren't snobbish about tropes.

That's only writers (and maybe fans of literary fiction, who probably aren't your audience – at least, not if you want to write a bestseller).

Readers love books that give them something familiar.

Imagine somebody loves reading Ian Rankin, for example, or maybe James Patterson or Sara Paretsky. They'll also enjoy reading other books that work in a similar way.

They won't think you've copied those other authors; they'll just enjoy the fact that they're reading something familiar. One of the most powerful ways to sell books is 'if you enjoy x, then you'll love y'. Big publishing houses do it all the time.

Forget all the snobbery and preconceptions about tropes. Throw them out the window and then do your research on those tropes.

How to research genre tropes

How do you do the research?

The first method is to read books in your genre, and lots of them.

Compare how they work, identify the key points in the story. Try to spot the tropes and how they've been made fresh.

Find the top 20 books in your genre right now. Even better, find the top 20 using the same publishing route as you, because you can learn more from them.

If you're an indie, identify the top selling indies – and maybe the top sellers from digital-first publishers too, as they share methods and markets.

If you're looking for a deal with a big publisher, find the big sellers from those publishers.

Read them carefully. Make notes. You might even go so far as to create a spreadsheet, like I did.

Think about the characters, the settings, the plotlines, the subplots, the world building, the use of language. Make more notes.

Next, read reviews. What's in the one-star and the five-star reviews? Two-star reviews can also be useful, because one-star reviews are often more about the reviewer than they are about the book. Find out what readers love and hate about these books. It might be the same thing, which will tell you something about how effectively that book was targeted at the right audience.

For example, when I researched police procedurals, I discovered from reviews that there were two elements to the books that are actually more important than the mystery: the characters, and the setting. That surprised me. But it meant that I set out to write compelling characters that readers wanted to get to know, and it made me think of my setting as being like an extra character. The mystery needs to be credible and compelling, but that alone isn't enough.

What you learn will be different for your genre, but avoid making assumptions before you start. By knowing what readers really love reading, you'll be in a much better position to give them something they love, and have much more chance of writing a bestseller.

12

RESEARCHING THE MARKET

In 2018, I came up with an idea for a series of mysteries.

It was a sci-fi cozy mystery with a talking cat called Schrödinger, a team that travelled through the multiverse to investigate parallel crimes, and a lesbian romance.

I researched all the genres it could slot into – animal cozy mystery, time travel (sort of) sci-fi, lesbian romance, and they were solid genres. I thought I had a potential hit on my hands.

Of course, I didn't. And the reason was that by trying to hit too many genres, I didn't hit any of them in a way readers responded to. The series was impossible to market because there was no clear target audience and no good comps. I quit writing that series after the second book flopped (it sold 42 copies compared to 300 for the first book, a clear sign that I'd done something wrong).

We've already talked about how you need to get to know your genre, so that you know what the tropes are and can understand what it is that readers will react to.

But there's another way in which you need to know your genre. And that's the market.

Your book will sit within a specific segment of the book market. It may sit in more than one segment, but it pays to understand where your book will fit.

This applies whether you're seeking to be traditionally published, or self-published.

Agents and publishers like to know that their authors understand where their book fits, and which other books they can be compared to.

And if you're indie, you'll need to market your book to readers of that genre. Which means knowing who they are and where to find them.

WHEN I DECIDED to start writing crime, I put a lot of effort into understanding the market for crime books in the UK.

Firstly, I realised that there are two types of crime, which I've already discussed in the previous chapter.

(To recap, there's cozy mystery and police procedural.)

I chose to write police procedurals because I like to write suspense, and I also write characters who swear.

I then researched the market for police procedural novels in the UK and the US, since those were the two markets I had the best access to.

Crime is an unusual genre, in that it's huge in both the UK and the US, but there isn't as big a crossover between the two as you might think. This applies particularly if you're writing UK-based crime. Readers in the US love to read UK-based cozy mysteries, as well as American cozy mysteries, but they're not so keen on British police procedurals.

This has been borne out by my experience of selling books. I sell 95% of my books in the UK.

But that's not a problem, because the UK market for police procedurals is huge. Many, many millions of books are sold in my genre every year in the UK alone. And there are markets in Australia, New Zealand, and Canada, as well as in translation, particularly in Germany, where the book market is the largest outside the USA.

Before I started writing, I spent time getting to know who else was writing books in my genre, what was selling and what was moving up and down the charts.

I looked at the different publishing models. I identified the authors with big traditional publishers, the authors who were self-published like me, and the authors who were with the newer digital-first publishers. I knew that I could follow what those publishers were doing as well as the successful indies.

I then identified half a dozen authors who were selling very well in my genre, and who were using a publishing model that compared to my own. I looked at how many books they had available, how frequently they published, how long they'd been doing it for, and how long it had taken them to get established.

I read their books, to understand what readers loved about them. I followed them on social media. I used all this to inform my writing and my marketing. But I didn't copy. You'll see new authors thinking they can ape the success of another author by copying their covers or using similar titles. Even by duplicating their books with different character names (it has happened). It won't work – don't waste your time.

Instead, find the nugget of what works and build on that to create your own version of success.

. . .

When I was starting out in crime, I'd only written thrillers before, so I had to learn all this. I took two months off writing to do it, but it was worth it.

But market research is something I've never stopped doing. I'm constantly looking at the Amazon charts – for crime and for my subcategories. I know who's guaranteed to sell well with a new release. I know who's up and coming. I know who the massive names are, the people who may not release so often, but when they do, they've a sure-fire hit. I also know which publishers are growing their share of the market and are worth watching to learn how they do that.

If you're wondering whether you could hire someone to do this research for you, I would say don't. You need to do the research yourself – because only by doing this research, will you really understand the market and how you can best respond to it in order to become a best seller.

It's nuanced. It's different for every book and every author. And the closer you are to it, the better use you can make of the information.

Top tips for understanding your market

Here are some things I do regularly that help me to keep abreast of what's going on in the market for books like mine:

1. Check the Amazon charts weekly, if not daily. Look at your subcategories and identify what's selling. Is it changing? Can you take advantage of that?
2. If you're looking for a trad deal, check out your

local bookshop(s). Find out what's on the front tables. Chat to the booksellers and find out what they're expecting to be big. Build a relationship with them, because one day you might want them to promote your books.
3. Follow the bestselling authors in your genre. Find their websites and sign up to their newsletters. Follow them on Amazon, BookBub, Facebook, Twitter, Instagram – wherever they are. Watch what they're doing, and what works.
4. If an author is advertising on Facebook, you can see their ads via the 'Page Transparency' section of their page. Google how to access it and see what ads they're running.
5. Look at the also-boughts and the sponsored carousel at the bottom of book pages on Amazon. What's there? What makes you want to click? Which books have just appeared? And which books do you keep seeing?
6. Join communities of readers. Find groups on Facebook (and elsewhere, if relevant) for fans of your genre. DO NOT use these groups to talk about your writing – you'll come across as sleazy. Instead, engage with the conversation about what people are reading. Find out what they love, and why. And build relationships.
7. In particular, look for change. Is there a new subgenre opening up that you could write in? Have indies recently started making inroads into your genre? Is there a new publisher you could submit to?

GET INFORMED before you put your book out there, and don't stop once it is out there – even after you become a bestseller. The more knowledge you have, the better you'll do.

13

RESEARCHING STORY AND CRAFT

We've already discussed genre tropes and the specific elements that you might find in a book in your genre.

But below all that is another, deeper, layer. And that's the layer of story.

Writing compelling stories is incredibly hard, in my view. It's harder than writing beautiful prose.

If you write a book that's a little bit clunky and needs a good edit, it's not a problem. You can come back to it, go over it time and time again and fix that prose. You can polish it till it shines.

But if your book doesn't have a solid story from the outset, there's little you can do to fix that. To be honest, if you don't get the story right on the first draft, the chances of you getting it right later are slim, and you might as well start again.

This is why researching what makes great stories is important. There are two ways to do this. Let's look at each of them in turn.

Read – lots

Like most writers, I've been reading since I was old enough to hold up a book.

I remember going on holiday to France and having to drive across the border to Geneva because I'd run out of reading material and needed to find the nearest English language bookshop.

Historically, when I flew, half my weight allowance was taken up by books (I am so grateful for the Kindle).

These days, my Kindle goes everywhere with me. It stays in my bag, and I get it out whenever I'm waiting for something. If I'm sitting on a train or at a bus stop, or I'm waiting for my kids to come out of school.

I hope that you're like me.

I very occasionally meet people who want to be writers, but don't read. I can't get my head around it. Why would you expect other people to read your writing if you don't read yourself?

The best way to learn how to be a writer is to read. That's how you learn how it's done. Don't read the books that your teachers told you to read at school. Read books that are fun to read. Books that are pacey and well-plotted. Books with fantastic characters who leap from the page and make you care about them. Books *you* want to read. Books that other readers are responding to: books that have created a stir.

Because it's only by reading books that are hugely successful that you'll understand what makes a story tick, and what readers respond to.

Read books in your genre, but not exclusively. Get a feel for the common threads between different genres and the underlying skeleton of a great story.

Read carefully. Watch for story beats that make you laugh, cry, and want to keep turning the pages. Identify what it is about the characters you love. It'll all help you become a better writer.

Books need structural beats and a firm skeleton. The jury is out on exactly what that looks like. And you'll probably pick it up by osmosis as you read. But just in case, there are always craft books.

Read craft books

As well as simply reading and picking up how to write by osmosis, you can also read books that will give you tips on how to structure your stories, how to write better characters, and just about everything else. Theme, plot, style: there's a book for everything.

I've got a bookshelf full of craft books. I regularly read new craft books, to pick up ideas and hopefully improve my own writing. But the more experienced I get, the less useful I find those books are. I've taken on board the advice in the best books, and I've also developed my own style and my own approach to creating a story.

I've read lots of craft books, and I don't slavishly copy any of them. Instead, I've experimented with ideas and figured out what works for me.

Over time, you'll cherry pick the nuggets of advice that appeal to you, mash them all together, and add your own method. That's what makes you unique as a writer.

But the advice that you get from some of those craft books can be incredibly useful. At the end of each section in this book, I've provided a list of resources – and that includes some of my favourite books on the craft of fiction.

Do a course – maybe

Another option when it comes to learning craft, is taking courses.

These might be short courses from as little as a day long, with seminars over Zoom or YouTube, to full-blown qualifications that require years of hard work to achieve.

They can be expensive, and you'll have to do plenty of research before you choose one. Make sure it fits with the style of writing you want to develop. Many of the most formal courses are quite literary, but that is changing. If you want to write genre fiction, make sure the course leader doesn't look down on it.

A course can be useful, but only if you put the work in. Personally, I've chosen self-guided study using a combination of reading, talking to other writers, and practising. Practice is the most important part. But if you need the impetus of being surrounded by other students or having an expert lead the way, then a course may be useful for you.

So, that's how you research story craft. In the next section of the book, I'll look at craft in more detail. I'll show you how I developed my craft in a way that was targeted at writing books readers loved and becoming a bestseller, and how you can do the same.

14

RESEARCH RESOURCES

Here are some of the resources on research that have been helpful for me.

Books

- *Six Figure Author* by Chris Fox
- *Write to Market* by Chris Fox
- *Strangers to Superfans* by David Gaughran.

Websites

- K-lytics - analyses the state of the Amazon book market every month in granular detail

PART III
STEP THREE - CRAFT

15

THE IMPORTANCE OF CRAFT

If you're aspiring to become a full-time author or even a bestseller, you've probably been working on your craft for a while. For most of us, that's what we start with.

I've been creating stories for decades. Before I ever thought about publishing a book, I wrote short stories. I wrote the occasional poem, probably (definitely) not very good. And I wrote a few short novels before I sat down and attempted my first 'proper novel'.

Before I published that novel, I wrote about ten drafts. The first one was dreadful. The next eight weren't much better.

But this is why it's important to work on your craft before you can expect to be successful.

When we start writing, we don't really know what we're doing. We have to learn. And while we can learn some of that from reading books, the best way to learn how to do something, is by doing it.

In this section of the book, I'm going to talk about how I

improved my craft and you can improve yours too. But importantly, I'm going to look at how you can focus your improvements on becoming a commercially successful author. In other words, instead of simply writing better books, learn to write books that readers love.

The focus of this book is on writing books that readers can't get enough of, which is the most reliable way to become a bestselling author. So read on, and find out how to write not just for yourself, but for readers too.

16

THE VENN DIAGRAM OF CRAFT

Finding the right kind of book to write involves a little bit of maths when it comes to craft.

When I started out, I simply wrote the story that was burning to get out of me. It was a complex political thriller that examined issues of family loyalty, global politics, racism, and misogyny. It was a huge, complex, sprawling monster with multiple timelines and way too many details. I didn't yet know how to write anything else.

That book eventually became four different books, each of which explored themes from the first book. But even after I'd split it into four books, they were books *I* wanted to write. Not necessarily books readers wanted to read.

There's nothing wrong with writing the book you're burning to write. I'm glad I wrote those books. I got them out of my head and onto the page, and I got some of my ideas out into the world.

But if you only write for yourself, it'll be much harder to become a bestseller.

Sure, there are some people who do it, but they're outliers. If you're strategically working towards writing books that sell and give you a writing career, you need to consider other people and not just yourself. And not just *some* other people. Every book, however obscure its niche, will have an audience of some kind. But if you're aiming for bestsellers, you don't want an audience of *some* sort. You want a big audience.

And that's where the Venn diagram of craft comes in.

THE VENN DIAGRAM of craft has three elements:

- what you love to read
- what readers love to read
- what you're good at writing.

What you love to read

I've already said in this book that writers tend to be more eclectic than the average reader when it comes to our reading habits.

But generally, we still have our own preferences. I'm much more likely to read thrillers and dystopian fiction than I am to read science fiction or fantasy. I rarely read romance. I love reading literary fiction that explores alternate realities, books like *Station Eleven* and *The Handmaid's Tale*, the sort of dystopian stories you can imagine actually happening.

The first few books I wrote were just like that: they were inspired by those books.

But there were two problems. I was inspired by literary

fiction, while not being a literary author. And even if I had been more literary in my style, those books would have been hard to sell.

I also enjoy reading thrillers and crime, anything with suspense, a sense of mystery and at least one twist. And I came to realise that if I wrote books like that, I'd be much more likely to succeed (more of which shortly).

Take some time to think about what you love to read. If you're writing a book, you're going have to read it quite a few times. And if you're writing something you'd enjoy reading yourself, it makes it much more enjoyable.

It doesn't have to be your very favourite type of book. But make a list, and then use the next two sections of the Venn diagram to whittle it down.

What readers love to read

The second section of the Venn diagram is what readers love to read.

Because if people don't love reading your books, then you'll have a struggle trying to sell them, whether that's direct to readers, or to publishers or agents.

For me, those dystopian thrillers just didn't have a big enough market. Some of them had female protagonists and were targeted at women, but were shelved in categories mainly read by men. So, for example, I wrote a trilogy of political thrillers that were similar to a Jeffrey Archer or a Michael Dobbs book, the sort of British political intrigue that you don't really see anymore. These days, political thrillers tend to be more action-oriented and targeted at men.

I was way off in terms of my target audience. I was

writing a book aimed at a group of people who didn't read that sort of book, trying to mix and match what I loved with what I hoped other people loved, and jam them together into a pattern that didn't really exist, however much I wanted it to.

All of which meant that no one was reading my books. And that's why I didn't become a bestseller.

But when I decided to switch to crime, which overlapped with what I love reading, I very quickly realised that there was a huge audience for those books. I wanted to write books with female protagonists, because I feel more comfortable writing female point of view characters. And there's a vast female audience for crime: in fact, James Patterson has said that more women read his crime books with male protagonists than men do.

Depending on your genre, that will be different. Which is where the research comes in. If you know who your target audience is and what they love, then you can gear your writing towards that.

But we're not done yet. What if you love reading sci-fi, and you know there's an audience for it, but you also know you aren't very good at world-building? You can either force yourself to learn, or you can pay attention to the third element of the Venn diagram.

What you're good at writing

The final factor in the Venn diagram is where your skills lie. Understanding that will help you write great books that keep readers coming back for more.

What I'm best at writing is suspense. I love writing scenes that make readers tense, and desperate to know what happens next. I also love throwing in unexpected twists.

I'd been using these techniques in my semi-literary thrillers, and getting good feedback on them. But where would it have more impact?

I'd already decided I wanted to write mysteries. But of the two main genres, it was obvious that police procedurals would give me more opportunities to write suspense than cozy mysteries. What suited me was writing dark, gritty stories. Even when I write in my rural Dorset Crime series, I make the locations atmospheric and brooding rather than idyllic.

In a cozy, you're more likely to find comedy and cute relationships, which can be a lot of fun to write, but which aren't my strength.

If you're not sure what you're good at, get feedback. Ask your writing critique group if you have one. Look at your reviews, if you're already published, and see what the readers liked – and what they didn't. Thank about what sections of your books make you feel proud. And then identify how you can use those skills to write books readers love, and that you love too. Because it's all very well learning to do something that doesn't come naturally, but you'll be much more successful if you play to your strengths.

* * *

FOR ME, that sweet spot in the Venn diagram was crime: I enjoyed reading those books, there's a huge audience for them, and I was good at building suspense.

So in early 2020, I started writing crime novels. It was a good move: those books sell over ten times what my earlier thrillers did.

By writing crime, I've been able to become a full-time writer, creating stories that I love writing and that readers devour. And when it comes down to it, that's the whole point.

17

IMPROVING YOUR CRAFT

In the previous section, I talked about researching story, structure and story craft, and how you can do that by reading plenty of stories, as well as craft books.

But as I've already said, the very best way to get better at your craft is to practise it. And that means writing: thousands, maybe millions of words.

Most of the successful writers I know didn't find success overnight. Sure, it might have looked like that, but in reality they'd been building their craft for years.

Look closer, and you'll often find that sudden success is anything but. A writer whose debut novel is a runaway hit might have been a journalist for years, or have unpublished books no one knows about. A writer who switches genres and suddenly starts to sell may have written dozens of books in other genres.

Being a great writer takes practice. You can't expect to do it overnight. Don't be so hard on yourself if your writing isn't as good as the books you're reading. Keep practising - and make that practice targeted.

. . .

THESE ARE the aspects of craft that I worked on when I started being more strategic with my writing.

Avoid flab

It's quite common for writers who quickly find success to have been writers of another kind before. I was a freelance technical writer before I turned to fiction. You'll find plenty of journalists or comedy writers turning to books and selling by the bucketload.

Those professions don't teach you to write stories, but they do teach how to write well, and sparingly. For a journalist or copywriter, not a word can be wasted. For a comedy writer, every word must be in service of the laugh. And for genre fiction, the same applies. You don't want flab.

Readers of genre fiction aren't looking for wordy descriptions that don't add anything to the story or to the world. What they're looking for is prose that helps them sink into the world or the story.

How spare your writing is will depend on your genre, and reader expectations (here's where your research comes in again). If you're writing thrillers, you'll have noticed that authors like Lee Child write tightly, with spare, lean writing that has very little exposition. If you're writing epic fantasy, you'll know that the big names like George RR Martin use more descriptive language to build the world of the story. But a good world-builder doesn't spend any longer doing this than they have to, and where they can, they build the world through action and dialogue instead of lengthy exposition.

Ditch those authorial tics

We all have them: little tics in our writing that we know aren't helping the story but that we just can't avoid.

I've now written twenty novels, and I've had them all professionally edited. Each time, I learn something new. My editor picks up on my bad habits and corrects them. Sometimes it takes me a few books to pay attention and stop doing it. And sometimes I'll argue with my editor, because I'm doing that thing deliberately (we disagree on use of the subjunctive). But through reading the feedback from my editor, and putting it into place, and putting it into action, I've become a better writer. I'm sure my editor will tell you that each book is easier to edit because I've learned.

That's not to say I'll ever be a 'perfect' writer. Nobody becomes a perfect writer.

But with every book you write, you become a better writer. And readers will notice.

This is one of the reasons that I start a new series every year. I want to give people a new starting point that showcases my improved skills, instead of expecting them to start with the very first book I wrote.

Three-dimensional characters

When I researched my genre and discovered that the thing readers responded most to was character, I worried.

I knew that my strengths weren't in character development. I preferred plotting, creating suspense, and exploring big ideas.

But although this wasn't a strength, I couldn't ignore it. So, I set out to improve my character development skills. I read books by authors who are great at characters and I took notes. I created character sheets for my characters so I got to know them better. I did psychometric tests for them. I even had imaginary conversations with them (only when no one else was in the house).

I also identified that I was better at writing sidekicks than protagonists. And so for my second series, I took a sidekick from the first series, and made her the protagonist. It worked: I love writing her, and readers tell me they love reading her. I'm going to do the same with another sidekick for my next series.

Character development is something I'm still learning, but I've spent time identifying the specifics of what I need to get better at, and making the effort to do it. If you love writing characters, then you won't need to do all this. But if you don't, it's something you can't avoid.

Compelling, coherent stories

Characters may be what people talk about in most reviews, but without a good plot, readers won't get to the end of a book.

Creating a good plot doesn't need to involve convoluted plans and multiple beats. What it boils down to is creating a series of events that are coherent and believable. X should lead to Y, rather than simply being followed by Y. The more influence the characters have on your plot, the better.

I'm lucky in that plotting has never been something I struggle with, but that doesn't mean I don't have to work at it. My readers would never finish my crime books if the crime itself didn't hang together, and in my books, the crime is the main focus of the plot. I also love writing longer, character-driven subplots that run throughout the length of a series. Mine will often involve intrigue and another layer of mystery, such as the death of a key character or suspected police corruption. If you can do this, it'll keep readers coming back to the next book in the series.

If you're not comfortable with plotting, try writing short stories for a while. That way, you get to create multiple plots without having to write multiple novels. The story may be shorter, but the same rules of story still apply. Once you're happy with plotting, switch to novels: it's very hard to make a living from short stories.

Zinging dialogue

A page-turner will often include a fair amount of dialogue, so it's important to get it right. Dialogue should reflect the characters – try removing the speech tags to see if you can still work out who's talking. See it as part of the action instead of exposition – use it to move the story along rather than just explaining things. Depending on your genre, dialogue can also be funny, shocking or inspiring.

The key is finding the balance between dialogue that's believable and dialogue that's too much like real life. Avoid having your characters constantly address each other by name, take out the 'yeah', 'so' and 'y'know's, and keep the dialogue as tight as the rest of the text.

Like everything else, the best way to learn dialogue is to read books that get it right. Another good technique if you want to hone your dialogue is to try writing a screenplay (or if you don't want to go that far, read some screenplays).

* * *

BUT THE ONLY SURE-FIRE way to get good at all this is by doing it again and again. Write, regularly. Practise your skills on short stories. Get feedback and use it in your next story. By editing your own work, by asking other people to give you feedback, and by working with professional editors, you will slowly but surely become a better writer.

THE MORE BOOKS YOU WRITE, the better you'll get. And don't listen to people who tell you that if you write a lot of books, you must be a hack. People will use phrases like 'churn out books'. Ignore them.

In no other profession is it considered bad to be prolific. Musicians who produce lots of music aren't derided. Prolific visual artists aren't considered worse than artists who just produce one artwork a year. The only reason people think of fiction like this is because traditional publishing houses have told us to. They have a one book a year system, so they've perpetuated the myth that one book a year is the best way to write. Ignore them and write at your own pace.

WRITE EVERY DAY YOU CAN, however many words you can, even if it's only a couple of hundred. Instead of using what you learn to rewrite the last story, apply it to the next one. Learn from your mistakes and identify ways in which you can improve your craft with every new story that you write. That way, you'll have a much better chance of writing a great book or series that lets you quit the day job.

18

HOW TO WRITE A PAGE TURNER

The key to an author career isn't writing one bestseller. It's writing multiple bestselling books.

And the best way to do that is to make people want to read not just one, but all of your books. One way to maximise your chances is to write in series (something I do). Another way is to make sure that everybody who picks up one of your books will finish it. After all, if they don't finish that book, they're not going to read another one.

The authors who sell big and have guaranteed bestsellers are generally those who can write page-turners. Books you don't want to put down (even if you secretly hate yourself).

There's a lot of snobbery around page-turners. People will tell you they hated a book, but couldn't stop reading it. Did they really hate it so much, if they couldn't put it down?

And writing page-turners isn't as easy as people like to think it is. After all, if it was, then we'd all be doing it.

. . .

So how is it done? What are the techniques that you can use to help ensure that your readers keep on reading?

In this chapter, I'll outline the methods I use to get my readers turning the pages. My reviews show that these are effective. I get emails from readers telling me my books kept them awake all night, and they couldn't put them down. (I always commiserate, but I'm secretly delighted.)

When I decided to get serious about my writing career, some of the research that I did was around page-turners and what it was that made people want to keep reading. I read the authors who are famous for writing those kinds of books. I read Dan Brown, I read (yes, from start to finish) EL James, and I read James Patterson. I picked up some of the tricks and techniques that they use to help readers race through their books.

Stirring the reader's emotions

When you read the reviews for books that sell by the truckload, they tend to refer to emotions.

With romances, readers will describe how their hearts raced when the protagonists got together. With thrillers, people will tell you how they found themselves on the edge of their seat. Science fiction and fantasy readers will discuss how they were swept away by this strange new world.

One technique to make sure that readers keep on reading your book is to aim for an emotional response rather than an intellectual one. Intellectual responses are all very well, but intellectual books are rarely bestsellers.

If you want to write a book that sells in the tens of thousands or even the millions, then find ways to tweak your readers' heartstrings.

To find out how to do it, read books that elicit an

emotional response in you, and identify what it was in those books that stirred that response.

Chances are, it'll be about characters and the situations the writer puts them in. Showing and not telling will be important, as well as using language that pulls the reader in. There'll be risk, jeopardy and high stakes, and an ending that makes the readers scream, sigh or swoon. And the plot must be both intelligible and accessible.

Find out how the successful authors in your genre elicit emotional responses. Identify the emotions you want to stimulate. And try it out in your stories.

Characters that jump off the page

When I researched the reviews for bestselling crime books, there was one thing that jumped out at me time and again (not literally), and that was the characters.

People didn't seem to care much for the mystery. They didn't worry about the writing style. But what they talked about was the characters.

If you can write characters that your readers engage with and want to know more about, then they'll race to the end and they'll be more likely to pick up the next book. Characters need to jump off the page and feel real – you want your readers talking about them as if they know them.

Take time to develop your characters before you start writing. Think about how they'll evolve over the course of a series. Identify what makes them special and what will make readers warm to them. Avoid stereotypes, and don't make them too perfect.

If your characters come alive in your own head, you're halfway there – they'll also make your readers feel like that. I have to admit I sometimes think of my characters as my imaginary friends, and I enjoy spending time with them. If your readers do too, they'll keep reading, because they will *care* about what happens to those characters.

Prose that doesn't draw attention to itself

I grew up thinking that the most important thing about writing was the quality of the prose.

How wrong I was.

It's tempting to spend hours polishing our words until they shine. Writing the sort of stuff our English teacher would be proud of.

But the reality is, readers aren't keen on that sort of prose. Yes, there is a place for beautiful prose, and that's in literary fiction. But – let's repeat it – it's very difficult to sell literary fiction. Most literary authors (including the ones who win awards) have another source of income.

When I spent time reading the bestsellers in my genre, I noticed that the prose was simple. It was prose that did one thing: it told the story. It didn't draw attention to itself. It didn't require you to think too hard. It just flowed. It was almost like the story was going straight into my brain without the words getting in the way.

James Patterson has sold over 300 million books. The prose in his books can be read by someone with six years of formal education: in the UK, that's a ten-year-old. That doesn't mean his books aren't suitable for adults: the content is very adult. But it does mean that anyone can read his prose, and they don't have to think hard to do it.

You might think that this kind of writing is dumbing down, and that writing simple prose is too easy. But if it is, why doesn't everybody do it?

The reality is that writing free-flowing, readable prose

that doesn't draw attention to itself is harder than you might think. It takes skill, good editing, and the ability to say no when you're tempted by highfalutin words.

Try reading some of the bestsellers in your genre, and looking at the style in which they're written. See if you can adapt your own style to make it simpler for people to read.

Here are some things that can work:

- short sentences
- short paragraphs (very important, as big blocks of text can be daunting to read)
- simple words instead of fancy ones
- no adverbs, and adjectives only when necessary.

Try editing your work to make it simpler, and see how much quicker you can read it yourself. The same will apply to readers. A bestseller won't slow them down.

Chapter length

When I set myself the challenging of reading a ton of bestselling crime novels, one thing I noticed was how short the chapters are. They'll almost always be less than 1000 words long, sometimes as short as 500 words.

Until I'd conducted that research, I'd been writing long chapters, on the advice of my first editor (who didn't normally work with genre fiction). My books had thirty or so chapters in them, which meant that each chapter was about 2,600 words long. In a paperback book, that's ten pages.

This might not seem like a lot. But when a reader comes to the end of a chapter, and the next one is ten pages long, they might think they don't have time for it. They'll put the book down. If a reader comes to the end of a chapter and the next one is 800 words long, they'll think 'this'll only take a couple of minutes' and they'll read on. If you write that chapter well, they'll go through the same thought process again. And again. Until it's 4am and they're sending you an email about how you kept them up all night.

This way, the reader ends up reading much more than the 2,600 words of the longer chapter. And you've created a page-turner.

There's another benefit to writing short chapters, and that's that they're well-suited to writing sprints. It takes me ten minutes to dictate a 1,000-word chapter. If I were typing, it would take me 25 minutes. Something I can easily squeeze into my day.

If you struggle with short chapters, try finding cliffhangers or breaks in the action. Switch between different characters doing things at the same time (I do this a lot). And read writers who do it – identify where they break their chapters. You don't have to leave out important detail: just split it into multiple chapters.

***

THESE TECHNIQUES WILL HELP you write page turners, but they aren't a quick fix. Add them onto everything you've learned about craft, plotting and characterisation and you'll create a book readers race through – and that makes them immediately buy the next one.

19

CRAFT RESOURCES

Here are some of the resources on craft that have been helpful for me.

Books

- *Into the Woods* by John York
- *Inside Story* by Dara Marks
- *How to Write a Novel Using the Snowflake Method* by Randy Ingermason
- *Save the Cat!* By Blake Snyder
- *Write to Market* by Chris Fox
- *The Story Grid* by Shawn Coyne

Podcasts

- The Story Grid Podcast

Newsletters

- Jericho Writers newsletter – Harry Bingham's weekly update has some great advice on craft.

PART IV

STEP FOUR - LAUNCH

20

WHAT I MEAN BY LAUNCH

So far in this book, we've looked at the foundations for developing a bestselling book, series, or career.

Now, I'm going to get a bit more specific (although not too specific – I'm aware that your situation is always going to be different from mine). It's time to move on and put your book out into the world.

Scary, huh? But if you're ever going to be a professional author, you have to do it.

The manner in which you put your book into the world will depend on the route to market that you've chosen. And in the next chapter I'll examine the pros and cons of different ways of publishing your book. I'll also help you work out how to get your book into the best possible shape, so it has the best possible chance of success.

This is when you send your beloved little book out into the wilds. It's the point at which you make yourself vulnerable. Where you invite criticism, reviews and feedback. It can be scary, I know. But if you're ever going to have a bestselling book, you need to take this leap.

So let's move on to looking at the different ways you might choose to publish your book, and the pros and cons of each.

21

STOP! DON'T PUT YOUR BOOK OUT THERE TILL IT'S READY

You're probably waiting for me to get into the meat of this section.

You want to know how you're going to sell your book and become a successful author.

I want to stop you in your tracks.

Sorry.

I know this isn't what you were looking for.

But I also know from my own experience that once you finish your first manuscript (most people do finish a manuscript before they start thinking about what comes next), you'll be eager to press on.

You might be drawing up a list of agents to submit to. You might be forking out for an expensive course on book marketing.

Before you do any of that, pause and take the time to get your book in the best shape it can be in.

Submitting to agents is time-consuming. It can be demoralising.

Marketing is time-consuming. It's expensive. And most of all, it's risky.

So you need a solid product before you send your book out there.

In the previous sections I ran through how you build that product. If you skipped straight to this section, you won't get the benefit of this book.

Close down Facebook Ads Manager. Resist the temptation to go into the Amazon advertising dashboard. Put away the list of agents.

I want to give you the best possible foundation to make a success of your book, once you do start marketing.

If you haven't already worked through the first three steps, do so – and then come back here.

If you have, then great – let's dive in.

22

ROUTES TO MARKET

There are two main routes to market for your book or your books: traditional publishing and self-publishing (or indie publishing, as I prefer to call it). There's also hybrid, which is a mix of the two.

Some authors choose one or the other. Some choose to go hybrid. Which of these is appropriate will depend on you, and on your book. And you can switch between these routes during your career: between books or even for an individual book.

But it pays to understand the routes to market before you put your book out there, so you can pick the route that's most likely to make your book a bestseller.

Traditional publishing

Traditional publishing means you have a contract with a publisher, and they publish your book. They might have the rights to publish your book in all formats, including paperback, hardback, ebook, audiobook, and possibly TV and film. Or they might just have specific rights over one or more formats or territories (i.e. countries or languages).

Either way, it means they have the sole rights to publish and distribute your book in the formats and territories defined by your contract. No one else can publish the book in those formats and territories, including you.

Many new authors sign a very broad publishing contract, handing over rights to all formats, languages and territories. Before you sign a contract like that, think about whether you might want to sell specific rights to other publishers or entities such as TV production companies, or whether you should retain some rights to publish yourself. It pays to research what standard terms are, how a contract works, what to expect and what's pushing too far before you sign your contract, even if you have an agent – more of which below – managing things for you. This is your career and your work, not theirs.

Many of the biggest publishers will only accept submissions from agents on behalf of authors. If you want to be published by one of those, you need to find yourself an agent first rather than a publisher. But if you're working with a smaller publisher or a digital publisher, you can often approach them direct. You'll need to do the research to find out which publishers are appropriate for you and your book, and how you access them.

Pros of traditional publishing

Historically, the biggest selling authors have been traditionally published, although that is changing. Let's take a look at some of the pros of getting a publishing deal.

. . .

Access to vast markets

It's true that many of the biggest hits in publishing are from the big publishing houses. The massive bestsellers that everybody's talking about are generally published by the big players.

If your publisher is passionate about your book, they will put marketing spend behind it. They will promote it to bookshops and make sure it's on the front tables. They might even advertise it on posters or billboards. They'll send it to reviewers and literary publications so that the word gets out.

PR like this is very expensive to do yourself and frankly, it's not worth it, because it's difficult to measure how effective it is. But if a book takes off, this kind of marketing can launch it into the stratosphere. But be aware that the vast majority of publishing deals don't come with this kind of marketing push, especially if the advance is small and the author isn't already a household name.

Less work

The other advantage of working with a traditional publisher is that there are aspects of the publishing process that you don't have to worry about.

The physical process of producing a book will be covered for you. Much of the editing, proofreading, etc. will be done, although you will be expected to respond to your editor's comments promptly. The covers will be dealt with on your behalf, and sometimes you won't even have the right to veto them.

Some of the marketing will be done for you, but these days, not close to all of it. Publishers tend to expect their authors to do quite a bit of marketing themselves. The reality is that those authors who do have the benefit of massive publicity campaigns and whose books are launched into the stratosphere are outliers. They tend to be established authors who've been with the publishing house for a while. But occasionally, you do see breakout successes.

So, if you don't feel that you have the skills or the mindset to publicise and market your book or to manage the publishing process, working with a traditional publisher could be the best route for you.

Cons of traditional publishing

There are some big benefits of letting a publisher handle your books for you, but there are downsides too.

Royalty rates

The biggest and most obvious downside of working with a publisher is that they keep most of the money. When your book sells, either through a bookshop or online, the publisher will take the royalty from that distributor and they will give you a percentage. Your agent, if you have one, will also take their cut.

Let's take a look at the maths. Imagine your ebook sells on Amazon for $9.99. The publisher will (most likely) get 70% of that from Amazon, and with most publishing contracts you'll get 25% of that.

Let's round it up to $10, for the sake of argument. The publisher gets $7 and you get 25% of that, which is $1.75. But you're not done yet. If you've got an agent, they'll get 15%. That means you'll end up getting $1.49. This is 14.9% of the price of the book.

If you're with a digital publisher, you might find your

royalties are higher. Many digital publishers pay 45% or even 50% on ebooks, so you could be getting up to 29.8% of the price of the book: $2.98, or, if you don't have an agent to pay, up to $3.50. But it's highly unlikely that a digital publisher paying a 45-50% royalty would be selling ebooks for anything close to $10 in the first place.

On paperbacks, royalty rates tend to be more variable and you have to factor in the cost of printing. It can mean that paperback sales can net you just pennies for each book. And if your book is discounted, for example if it's sold in a supermarket, you'll often get nothing from the sale. When you're signing a contract with a publisher, check for a discounting clause – make sure it doesn't reduce your royalty rate to zero because, believe me, that's common.

Lack of control

But money isn't the only downside with traditional publishing. For me, the main reason I'm indie is because I prefer to retain control.

With a traditional publisher, you have very little control over the fate of your book. You have little to no say over the title or cover. You'll have no say over the marketing plan and if there's a disagreement between you and your editor over editorial changes, then your opinion may not hold sway. When you sign your book over to a traditional publisher, it becomes their book and not yours.

Shelf-life

Many traditionally-published books burst into life, with broadsheet reviews, billboards and glamorous launches. It's a whirl. But look for that book a year later, and it'll have been forgotten. Sure, it might still be in Waterstones or Barnes & Noble, but you'll need someone's help to track it down. It'll still be on Amazon, but the most recent review will be from six months ago.

The business model for traditional publishing has always been driven by short-term sales, although this tendency is decreasing as series-driven fiction becomes more dominant. If there are no sales, or so few there might as well be none, the book should revert to you under the reversion clause, which allows for the contract to end in certain specified circumstances. Make sure you're happy with your reversion clause before you sign your book away!

No CONTROL over publishing pace

Traditional publishing is slow. If your book is picked up by an agent, it could be six months to a year before they sell it to a publisher. And then it could be eighteen months before it's published in hardback., Another year before the paperback comes out. That's three and a half years after you found your agent, maybe four years since you finished writing the book.

During this time, you'll wait months for editorial comments and then be given days to respond to them. The balance of speed is very much skewed against you.

Digital publishers are much quicker. They work directly with authors, and could publish your book within six months. They'll then want a book every three months. A better option if you write fast, but high pressure if you don't.

. . .

Now if you're happy with all that, that's fine. There are benefits that you get in return.

When traditional publishing works

I would suggest that the situations when traditional publishing is most suitable include the following:

Your book is literary fiction.

It's almost impossible to sell a literary book as an indie. It's a hard market to reach and one that's less likely to buy online. If you're literary, you'll need to find a publisher. You'll probably also need to accept that your chances of making a living from your writing are very low.

Your book is middle-brow (sometimes called book group fiction) and doesn't land squarely in another genre.

Again, these can be hard to sell as an indie but can do very well through a traditional publisher. You'll need to identify the publishers that are achieving success with this kind of book and work hard at hitting genre tropes, which aren't very well defined.

You're repulsed by the publishing and marketing process.

Some of us just aren't suited to running a small publishing business. Before you decide it's not for you, bear in mind that this isn't as daunting as you might think, and that there are plenty of resources out there and people to help you.

But if you really can't face the thought of doing this,

then handing over control to a traditional publisher will mean that you don't have to worry about this side of the process. But don't forget that you will still need to do some of the marketing yourself.

SEEING your book in bookshops is more important to you than money.
If you're an indie, it's very difficult to get your book into bookshops. Traditional publishers have people whose job it is to work with bookshop chains and get their books placed with them. If you're with a traditional publisher, your book is much more likely to appear on the shelves of your local bookshop, but remember it probably won't stay there for long after the launch month. But if you want your family and friends to be able to see your book on the shelves of your local Waterstones or Barnes & Noble, then traditional publishing could be for you.

Indie publishing

Indie publishing or self-publishing is when you retain all of the rights to your book, and publish it yourself.

This means working with distributors such as Kindle Direct Publishing (KDP), Ingram Spark, Kobo and others to upload your book and make it available for people to buy.

You'll have to manage all of the aspects of publishing yourself. You'll need to hire an editor and a proof-reader. You'll need to get the book formatted (which you can do with easily available software that's cheap or even free). You'll have to hire a cover designer and ensure you get a cover that sells the book. You'll need to write your own blurb. And you'll need to do all your own marketing.

If you've got a head for business, or you're keen to learn

about publishing, then indie publishing can be a lot of fun. I've thoroughly enjoyed learning about the publishing business and how to market my books. But in the early days especially, it can be a lot of work.

If you're happy to learn and you're excited by the idea of setting up a new business, then indie publishing could be for you.

Pros of indie publishing

I'm going to declare an interest here: I'm an indie, and I love it. Below are some of the benefits that means this route to publication appeals to me.

ROYALTY RATES

The biggest pro of indie publishing is that you get to keep a lot more money.

Let's take that ebook that's been sold on Amazon for $9.99. The reality is that as an indie, you're unlikely to sell it at such a high price point. Let's drop the price to $4.99 (still quite high for an indie) and take a look at what you get.

Amazon pays out 70% of that $4.99 (let's call it $5), which is $3.50, minus a small handling fee – so you'll probably get around $3.45, or 69% of the price of the book. That's $1.96 more than you'd get with a big publisher, even with the book at half the price.

But you also need to factor in the costs of producing and marketing the book. You'll need to pay your editor, proofreader, cover designer, and anybody you might hire to help with marketing. If you do the marketing yourself, you'll need to pay for ads.

But once your book becomes a bestseller, you'll find that

your expenditure becomes a lower percentage of your income. The costs of editing, cover design etc. are flat costs, no matter how many books you sell. And the more books you sell, the more of those sales will be organic, so you'll need to spend a much lower percentage on ads. (I cover organic sales in part 4 of this book.)

When I launched my Zoe Finch series I was spending around 40% of my income on ads. That seems like a lot. But by the time I had six books out I was spending just 20%, and getting ten times as many sales. Now I have four books out in my Dorset Crime series, I'm getting fifty times the sales and spending 10% of my royalties on ads. And the cost of production as a proportion of profits is much lower.

You can see that if your book (or more realistically, series) becomes a bestseller, there are big financial benefits to being indie.

Retaining control

The other big pro of being indie is the control you have over your career. This is probably the thing that keeps me indie publishing despite having had approaches from publishers. I can decide what I write and when I write it. I have control over which characters I introduce to my books. I have total control over the covers and the titles which means I can make sure that my books are very tightly branded across series. I can also decide to go back and make a strong marketing push for books I wrote years ago, which traditional publishing would have forgotten about. I'd struggle to give up that control.

Relationship with readers

The third benefit of being an indie is that you will often be closer to your readers, because there aren't so many people between you and the reader. With a publishing deal, you've got the agent and editor, the publishing house's sales department, and the bookshop. As an indie, it's just you and your readers.

I love talking to my readers. I get emails and messages from readers every day, telling me what they enjoyed about the books. I get feedback about specific characters and suggestions on what they'd like to see in future books. And if I want to, I can work those suggestions into those books, without a publisher being able to stop me.

Cons of indie publishing

That's not to say that self-publishing doesn't come without its downsides.

Risk

Indie publishing is quite risky.

If your books don't sell, then you'll have shelled out your own money for editing, cover design, etc. If you don't watch what you're doing, you can lose a lot of money.

There are also scammers who will con you into handing over cash to buy their publishing services. It's important to be able to differentiate between reputable and dodgy publishing services companies, and organisations like the Alliance of Independent Authors can help you with that.

You need to have your eyes wide open, and you need to do the work up front to maximise your chances of writing bestsellers and making a profit. Or you need to accept the risk.

It's a lot of work

The biggest con is probably the amount of work and learning you'll have to do to become a successful indie author.

You'll need to set up a publishing business, which means learning the ins and outs of the publishing industry. You'll have to find out how to bring a book from first draft to final product, and learn how to market books effectively.

It can all be daunting at first. But once you've done it a few times, it becomes very rewarding and much easier.

But you do need the right mindset to be able to cope with all that learning and extra work.

When indie publishing can work

Indie publishing works best in the following situations:

The book is genre fiction that clearly fits into its niche.
As an indie, most of your sales will be on Amazon. And if your book is similar to other books in the Amazon categories you're using, then the algorithm will kick in and it'll sell your book to people who read similar authors. This is why it's so important to understand your market. I learned to my cost that if your book doesn't fit into a genre, it's very hard to sell enough copies to make a living.

You're comfortable learning how to publish a book and create a polished product.
You'll need to learn how to create a book from your

initial draft. If you enjoy this, then great: you're suited to being an indie.

YOU HAVE a head for marketing and figures.

You'll need to do a lot of data analysis to identify which of your adverts are profitable and which aren't. If you're comfortable with spreadsheets and figures, you'll have an advantage. But if you aren't you can always learn – or hire the services of someone who is.

YOU LIKE to retain control over your books and your career.

If you can't bear the thought of a publisher or agent telling you what to do, then indie publishing might be the only route that'll make you happy. I know that applies to me!

YOU WRITE in series

Marketing a series as an indie is much easier than marketing standalones. It means you can push book 1 in your series and then use various techniques to encourage read-through, i.e. people moving through to the following books. The best way to improve your read-through is to write great books, and if you can get it to work it can be the cornerstone of a successful career.

NOTE: If you decide to see-publish, you'll then need to decide whether to make your books exclusive to Amazon or to go 'wide'. There are pros and cons to each and I'm not going to go into detail here as the land-

scape does change. But do your research - and remember that you aren't committed to either option forever.

If all of the above apply, you might want to go for indie publishing. It's the route I use and the one that I think gives you the best chance of making a living with your writing these days. However, there is a third option and that's to go with a combination of the two.

Hybrid publishing

Hybrid publishing is publishing your books through a combination of traditional and self-publishing. It can take two forms.

You can either publish some of your books using one route, and other books using the other. Or you can publish one book in different formats using the two different methods.

Publishing some books trad, some books indie

There are some authors who've established themselves with a traditional publisher and then decide to publish one or more books themselves. This might be because they can write faster than their publisher wants them to, or they have a series idea the publisher isn't interested in. It might be that they've looked at the profile their traditional publisher has built for them, and want to use it to sell their books more profitably. So they'll write some more books and publish them independently.

Alternatively, you'll find authors whose situation with their publisher changes. The rights to some or all of their books revert to them, and they start publishing them independently.

Yet more writers start out self-published, and then get a deal with a publisher when they achieve success.

Mixing trad and indie for one book
A lot of indie publishers are using hybrid routes for individual books.

So, for example, you might publish your ebook and paperback independently, but then choose to publish audiobooks or translations via a publishing company. Or any combination of formats and territories.

Hybrid publishing is incredibly flexible, and it's growing, as are the number of publishers and agents who are prepared to work with hybrid authors. Some of the newer publishers are very welcoming to hybrid authors and actively seek to work with authors who've been successful as indies.

Pros of hybrid publishing

Hybrid publishing is so flexible and varied that it's difficult to anticipate the pros and cons, as they'll differ for each author. But these are some of the most common advantages.

Publishing more books
If you previously found success with a traditional publisher, and you decide to publish some books indie, you've got an eager audience. Publishing more books will

keep those readers happy and get you more sales. And you'll keep more of the royalties.

Reaching a bigger audience

If you've previously self-published and you get a deal with a traditional publisher, you'll have access to a wider audience. You may find your books in physical bookstores when they weren't before, or find that the publisher can promote your books to people you haven't been able to reach. And for the publisher, they know there's an existing audience and less risk.

Less work

If you're an indie who works with a publishing company for specific formats, languages and/or territories, it can save you work and be less risky. You don't have the upfront costs of audiobook production or translations, for example, and can leave the publisher to take that risk. At the same time, you can continue to focus on selling your books to your core audience as an indie.

But it's worth remembering that if your book is successful in those formats and markets, you'll make less money this way. Pick your formats, languages and territories (and publisher) wisely.

Cons of hybrid publishing

Hybrid publishing can have its downsides too.

Potential extra work

The main downslide of hybrid publishing is the work managing it all.

You can find yourself torn in two, with your feet not quite in one camp and not quite in the other. You'll have to manage relationships with publishers and understand contracts as well as running your own publishing business.

But as long as you're careful choosing which books and/or formats you publish using which method, it can be a great way to get your books to the widest possible audience. And pick your publisher wisely too, especially if you're an established indie: don't forget that the publisher is trading on *your* name.

* * *

THERE YOU HAVE IT: the three main routes to market.

I'm not going to tell you which one will work best for you, because it will depend on your skill set and preferences, as well as on your book.

But before you put your book out there into the world, it's a good idea to get to grips with these different publishing models and work out which one is really the best for you. Not the one that your friends are doing or that people expect you to do, but the one that will maximise your book's chances of being a bestseller and making you a full-time living.

23

GETTING YOUR BOOK IN THE BEST POSSIBLE SHAPE

Before you put your book out there, whether that be by putting it up for sale or submitting it to agents or publishers, it's vital to get it in the best shape you possibly can.

THIS IS something I've worked hard on with my own books. I'm self-published, and not ashamed of it in the slightest. But I want my books to be indistinguishable from books published by Penguin Random House, HarperCollins or any of the rest of them.

I want readers to see my book on bookshop shelves or its Amazon product page, and instantly think 'that looks like a good book'.

That means having a professional cover and a blurb that hooks readers in and reflects the quality of writing inside. The reality is that if your cover looks cheap, people will assume your writing is just as bad. If your blurb is clunky, people will assume the book hasn't been edited. And if you're submitting to agents or publishers, you'll need to edit your book and make sure it meets their requirements. Don't expect your publisher to do all the editing for you. You'll also need to prepare a cover letter and synopsis, and make sure you do these well.

I'M GOING to touch briefly on how you get your book into the best shape possible before submitting it to agents, and then I'll spend longer looking at how a book can be presented professionally for indie authors, because you do have more control over book presentation as an indie.

Preparing your book for submission to agents and publishers

You MUST get your book in tip-top shape before submitting it. Don't just send your first draft and expect it to get picked up.

POLISH the book so it shines

When I wrote my first book eighteen years ago, I was lucky enough to have a work colleague who was also a professional fiction editor. She very kindly read my manuscript and made suggestions. (She covered it in pencil: the first draft was dreadful.) I remember asking her an embarrassingly rookie question. I asked her if I should wait until I'd made the edits before I submitted it to agents. She replied by email, and I'm amazed she stopped herself using all caps or throwing the manuscript at a wall in frustration. *Yes*, was the reply.

Agents and publishers will only be interested in books

that are in great shape. They drown under a deluge of manuscript submissions every day.

Get it edited. If you can't afford to pay a professional, ask someone with relevant experience: maybe another writer. Ask friends who read in your genre to beta read and give you feedback. Make changes. Take feedback. Work on it till it's as good as it can be.

Don't expect an agent or publisher to pick up a book with potential but needing a lot of work: that just means more effort. And even if they're only asking for the first five thousand words or fifteen chapters, you'll need to ensure the whole book is in the right shape, for two reasons: it's the whole book that will be reflected in your cover letter and synopsis, and if they do like your initial submission, they'll be coming back to you for the rest of it before too long.

Follow submission requirements

Agents and publishers will publish their requirements on their website and you must follow them to the letter. It doesn't matter if the requirements are different for every agent you're submitting to (hint – they probably will be): make the changes for each one. They want to know that you're a professional and that you're willing to work with them, not against them.

I'm not going to dwell on how to write the perfect submission covering letter, and the art of the synopsis: there are plenty of books and blogs out there telling you how to do this, and it would distract from the purpose of this book. But whatever you do, make sure you don't ruin all your great work on your book with a shoddy submission pack.

Preparing your book for self-publishing

Before you publish your book, you need to think of it as a product, and ensure that product is packaged professionally and in a way that'll make it more likely to sell. There are two main aspects to this: the cover and the blurb.

A PROFESSIONAL COVER

There's a cliché in the book world that people like to use when they're talking about book covers. I'm going to avoid using it here, because it drives me nuts.

But the reality is, your book's cover is the single most important thing that will help sell the book. Not the content, not the blurb, but the cover. Because if the cover isn't appealing, then people won't look at the blurb or the opening chapter.

Before people read the blurb, they will see the cover. They might see it in an ad, in a bookshop, or in an email from Amazon. If it does its job, it will make them want to know more.

And when I refer to an appealing cover, I don't mean a beautiful one. I mean one that tells the reader what to expect inside.

There are three aspects to this:

- What's inside is what the reader likes to read. Make sure the cover fits with the genre, and conveys what's inside. Test it on people: show it to them and ask them what kind of book it is. They should get it right, every time. Forget about standing out from the crowd or creating a beautiful piece of art (unless your genre calls for

art). Your cover is packaging. It should sell the book.
- What's inside is professionally written and edited. If the cover looks professional, then people will assume that the writing is just as good. No matter how good your story, if the cover looks like it was produced on the cheap, it'll put people off. The cover shouldn't make people think about the quality of the writing: a good one doesn't make people question that.
- The covers of your books are strongly branded, especially if you write in a series. It should be immediately apparent to readers that these books are by the same author and (if appropriate) in the same series. You can do this with fonts, positioning and style. Branding will increase read-through and help you sell more books to each reader.

Take the time to research covers in your genre and make sure yours is just as good, and fits with what readers expect.

A GREAT BLURB

The next thing people will look at after the cover is the blurb or description.

There are plenty of schools of thought on the best way to write a blurb and I'm not going to recommend any one of them here. You need to research what works in your genre and test multiple blurbs to see what works for you.

Remember that your blurb isn't a synopsis. It shouldn't describe the plot or the characters in detail, but instead give the reader a taste of what to expect. It should also hook them, by leaving questions unanswered. And again, it should be appropriate for its genre.

When you're learning how to write blurbs, use the blurbs of bestselling books in your genre as a guide. Try using the same buzzwords if they have them. Experiment with structure and hooks. You can change your blurb as often as you like, and test which version works. Or you can try using ads with different blurbs and see which of those get the most clicks. But don't assume that your first blurb is the one that's going to work.

If you're submitting to agents or publishers, you'll need to write a kind of blurb too, in your covering letter. You don't get a free pass - sorry.

Before I wrote the blurbs for my crime books, I trawled through the Amazon charts and identified the top 20 bestselling books in my genre. I copied out each of the blurbs and identified the buzzwords that were being used in each of them. These will vary according to genre: for crime they'll include words and phrases like *murder, killer, strike again, solve the crime, before it's too late*.

Now try fitting at least two of those into your own blurb. More if you can do it in a way that sounds natural. Like cover design, this will make the book feel familiar to readers and give them a sense of what to expect. And it will give you a better feel for how successful, similar authors are selling their books.

THE OPENING CHAPTERS

Once a reader has decided they like your cover and your blurb enough to try your book, you need them to be intrigued by the opening chapter, page or even sentence.

If somebody's standing in a bookshop, before they buy a

book they'll flip it open. If they're on Amazon they might click on the *look inside* feature or download a sample to their Kindle.

Either way, they're trying out your writing and seeing whether they like it. However many times you edit the rest of the book, I think it's worth giving the first chapter extra attention.

I tend to submit the opening chapters of my books to my writers' group for feedback. I ask them one question: does this chapter make you want to read on? That's all I care about. I want the opening chapter to interest a reader enough to buy the book. And if they've already bought it, a strong opening will make them keep reading.

So, make sure your opening chapter, paragraph and sentence are as strong as they can possibly be.

GETTING your book into tip-top shape before you send it out there is so important. If it looks professional and has been edited thoroughly, then you stand a much better chance of it being a bestseller.

The next step is to start getting sales. In the following chapter I'm going to look at how you can do that if you're an indie author.

24

STRATEGICALLY SEEDING BOOK SALES

If your book is going to be a bestseller, you won't be responsible for the vast majority of sales. Once a book gets to that stage, it's word of mouth and organic sales that make the difference.

But in the beginning, you need to seed those sales.

I did this strategically. I spent time researching the channels available to me and I did lots of testing.

This is what worked for me. But (and this is a big but), it won't work the same way for you. I hope that my experience can help you get a better understanding of how to kick off sales. I hope you can adapt my methods and tweak them to fit your own book and your own genre - because you've researched your genre, right?

I'm going to look at paid advertising and promotion here, because when you're a nobody and you want to get big sales, ads are the best way to do it.

You can use ads to get sales started, and you can use ads to feed data to Amazon. As Amazon is the biggest bookseller for indies, feeding it this data will encourage the system to sell your books for you. Which is how you create a bestseller.

Remember – ads won't work if your book isn't in prime condition. Do your research and make sure it's professionally edited with a great cover and blurb. Otherwise, you're throwing good money after bad.

Note: this is probably the most technical chapter of the book, but I've tried to avoid going into too much detail. If you want more information and advice on the specifics of advertising and marketing, I included a list of recommended books and courses at the end of this section of the book. It's also important to say that I'm going to describe what worked for me, with my first crime series launching in the summer of 2020. Your mileage may (will) vary.

What your ads should achieve

Your advertising should achieve three things:

- It should sell books. That goes without saying. You want to get a positive return on your ad spend. But effective ads will do more than just that…
- It should sell books to the right people. Avoid a scattergun approach to ads. If you target your ads at fans of similar writers (your 'comps'), and those people buy your book, then Amazon will learn that those people like your books. It'll have data it can use to start recommending your books to more of the right people. And then they'll be more likely to buy your book. Which leads me to…
- It should have a high conversion rate. When you start running ads, you'll be tempted to focus on

the cost per click. But when it comes to kicking off a bestseller, the conversion rate is more important. You want a high proportion of the people landing on your book's sales page going on to buy it. That way, the algorithm learns that your book converts well.... And it recommends it to yet more people.

If you can do these three things with your ads, you're on your way to a bestseller. I launched my Detective Zoe Finch series with Facebook ads for a single book on preorder. This runs counter to a lot of the advice you'll hear. But because I'd done my research and written a book I knew would work, and because I targeted those ads effectively, I was able to double my money – although it certainly helped that I knew I had plenty more books coming. And then when I released more books in the series, the ads became even more profitable.

Book advertising: the options

The four main advertising platforms for books are Facebook, Amazon, BookBub ads (NOT featured deals) and promotional email lists (not your own mailing list: that's a given).

I'm going to work through these in the order in which I used them to launch my series. I'm not saying the same thing will work for you, but it did work for me. I'll show you how each advertising platform helped me meet the three objectives above. But remember: you have to test ads yourself (with a low budget) to find out what works for you: nothing replaces your own testing.

Facebook ads

When I started selling my first crime series, I found that the best platform for getting things started was Facebook ads.

Warning: your mileage may vary. Don't assume that because it worked for me, it'll work for you.

Here I'll outline the strategies I used to sell books strategically using Facebook ads, so that Amazon then started picking up those books and selling them for me.

SELLING books with Facebook ads

Using Facebook ads to sell books profitably can be tough. Facebook will happily spend your budget for you, regardless of what your return on investment is. And like everything else, Facebook is constantly changing: its algorithm, its targeting, even its interaction with other tech platforms like Apple's iOS can impact the effectiveness of its ads.

If you're going to use Facebook ads, you need to start with a low budget and test meticulously to make sure that your ads are providing a positive return on investment. In other words, you want them to be profitable.

I started running Facebook ads for my first crime book when I put it on preorder in the spring of 2020. I started with a low budget, around $5 a day in total. I set up four versions of the ad using different images and text.

I tested these to work out which was the most effective with a broad audience. Once I'd found the version of the ad that was the most profitable, I started testing audiences: my comp authors. I was careful to split those authors out in different ads, so that I could see the impact of serving ads to different audiences.

Warning! If you're already advertising and/or you already have a readership, you'll have organic sales, meaning you can't attribute all your sales to ads. Consider setting up an Amazon affiliate account so you can track links.

Based on preorder sales and ad spend, I was doubling my money (a 100% return on investment). I was very happy with that, especially as it included breathing room for sales that weren't due to the ads.

So I carried on running ads using a low budget during the preorder period. And then once the book was released, I increased my budget. The ads became more profitable because I put a second book on preorder. I made the assumption that no one would preorder that without buying the first book, which meant I could calculate read-through. Read-through is critical: it tells you how many buyers of your first book go on to buy your second, third, fourth and so on; it can do the same with other formats, too, such as Kindle Unlimited page reads. As a result, it tells you the real value of a sale of book one, which can be a lot more than the 70% royalty you're getting directly from that sale.

I'm not going to go into detail here as to how you calculate read-through: I've listed resources later in this book that will help you do that, but it's important to calculate.

That's how I used Facebook ads to start selling books. What about selling books to the right people?

Using Facebook ads to sell books to the right people

Facebook ads aren't quite as effective as some of the other advertising platforms for micro-targeting comp authors. This is because you can only target the very biggest name authors on Facebook. I found that I couldn't target the indie and digitally-published authors I wanted to.

But if you're clever with your targeting on Facebook, you can find comps who are sufficiently similar to your books for your sales to start feeding the algorithm with useful information. I made sure I was only advertising to fans of crime fiction as well as specific crime authors. I only included those authors that were profitable, but by avoiding a scattergun approach I could start to provide also-bought data for Amazon.

This is critical: you want Amazon to know that people who bought your comp author *also bought* your book. The more people who do that, the more likely it is Amazon's AI will decide that it's worth recommending your book to readers of your comp author.

Selling to the right people means Amazon will start doing the selling for you. Selling to the wrong people means Amazon will either not bother selling for you, or will attempt to sell to readers who aren't that likely to be fans of yours. And it'll drive bad reviews, which nobody likes.

Running Facebook ads that convert

When you're testing your Facebook ads, make sure you measure conversions and sales, not just clicks. The Facebook dashboard will give you information on your clicks and the cost per click. And it's tempting to identify the best performing ad based on that data. But the reality is that an ad with cheap clicks might not be your best converting ad.

Creating high converting ads is important for two reasons. Firstly, it's more profitable. Secondly, it gives Amazon data that it uses to determine how likely your book is to convert when somebody goes to the book description page.

If your book converts well, Amazon is more likely to

recommend your book to people and push it for you. Make sure when you're testing your Facebook ads that you measure conversion and you pick the high-converting ads to run long-term.

BookBub ads

I don't spend a lot of money on BookBub ads because I find it difficult to make them profitable in my genre and with my target audience. They're incredibly competitive and I know some of my comps are spending a lot of money on them. That drives up the price of clicks, which means my ads have to convert incredibly well to be profitable.

Having said that, in the early days I did use BookBub ads to seed sales to the right people, as I'll explain.

Using BookBub ads to sell books

Whether you're able to make a profit from BookBub ads will depend on how low you can drive the cost of clicks. Conversion rates tend to be relatively high, although in my experience they're dropping over time.

People receiving the BookBub newsletter are looking for deals, so they're unlikely to click on an ad for a full price book unless it's a new release. If you want to use BookBub ads to sell books profitably, you need to work on your ads to get the cost of clicks down and maximise conversion.

I find that BookBub ads require more testing than any other platform because the margins are so tight. Take the time to hone your ads and your audiences. The audience for the BookBub email is huge, so if you can get it right, you can sell in vast quantities.

. . .

5 Steps to Author Success

Using BookBub ads to sell books to the right people

This is where BookBub ads really come into their own. When I launched my first crime book, I deliberately ran BookBub ads not to make a profit, but to provide Amazon with data.

I ran a series of BookBub ads to my closest comps around the time that my book launched. They made a slight loss, but I was prepared to take that hit because my goal was to give Amazon data on who was buying my book. I wanted those comps I'd targeted to be my also-boughts.

When I did this, I saw my also-boughts changing. The impact was mainly on the also-boughts on my author page: the list of authors on the left hand side of the page. I doubt that many readers use this to find new books, but the important thing is that it meant Amazon had the right data.

The algorithm was picking up on the fact that people who read my comp authors were also buying my book. And that was exactly what I wanted to achieve.

Running high-converting BookBub ads

Just like Facebook ads, you need to test not just clicks but conversions with BookBub ads. BookBub ads can convert well: they're going out to people who want books, after all. But this doesn't mean you can just assume your ads are converting.

Something not many people know is that when you set up a BookBub ad, you don't have to use the link that's automatically generated by BookBub. Instead, you can use an affiliate link to get data on how well your BookBub ads are converting.

Maximising your conversion rate again provides Amazon with data telling it that people who land on your books page tend to buy the book, and that means Amazon will be more likely to promote your book for you.

For me, this was less of an issue than targeting the right audience, but for you it might be a crucial factor.

Amazon ads

Amazon ads are very different from Facebook and BookBub ads. The focus is less on the creative element of it and more on the targeting. While Amazon ads can be very simple, if you're going to make them work you'll need to do more than set up an auto-targeted keyword ad and just hope for the best.

If you want to get to grips with Amazon ads, you'll need to understand the different ways of targeting and the levels within your campaigns.

There are multiple ways that you can target using keywords, products or categories. And within each campaign you'll be creating ad sets and individual targets. You can adjust the bid for each of those, meaning you could have hundreds of bid levels within one campaign. But the very fact it's so complicated means that if you can get it to work for you, you'll have an advantage.

Let's look at how I used Amazon ads for each of my three strategic goals.

USING Amazon ads to sell books

The biggest challenge in using Amazon ads is getting them to deliver in the first place.

Clicks can be very expensive, so bids need to be high. Even more of a problem is the fact that books that aren't already selling are difficult to get impressions for.

This is because Amazon has two sources of data when it's deciding whether to serve your ad. Unlike other advertising platforms, Amazon knows how well your book is already selling and how well it converts. As well as looking at the bid level, it will also look at how likely your book is to convert once someone clicks on the ad.

This is why I used other platforms first. I made sure that my books were selling at a healthy level and that my pages were converting well before I spent any money on Amazon ads. Having more than one book out also meant that I could bid higher, because of read-through. But I believe the biggest factor was the fact that Amazon already knew my books would sell.

Once your books are already selling, the biggest advantage of Amazon ads is that they convert in a way that Facebook ads don't. I can spend five times as much on Amazon ads as I can on Facebook ads before the cost per click starts to rise. Once your book is selling, they can be the best way to propel it into the charts and build sales that'll sustain a career.

USING Amazon ads to sell to the right people

Amazon ads can be incredibly powerful for doing this, because you can not only target specific authors, but specific books too.

When I started using Amazon ads, I targeted ASINs: specific ebooks written by my comps. I did this instead of using keywords because I wanted to make sure my ads weren't displayed on the pages of paperback books. If paperback readers click through to my book and buy it, my return on investment will be very low: ebooks are higher converting and more profitable for me, as for most indies.

This worked well for a while. But over time, the audience was too small for the number of ads I wanted to run. So I extended this out to targeting categories. This is what I do now.

Most people focus on keywords when setting up Amazon ads, but for me, ASINs and categories have helped me be more targeted.

Note: category targeting will only work if you can target categories in the Kindle store, not the overall book store. Check this is the case in the territory you're targeting.

I now target books in the same categories as my own books, which helps me sell books to the right people. If those ads convert, Amazon knows that people who buy books in that category will buy my books. Amazon will start pushing those books to people who buy from the category, and I'll start getting a lot more organic sales.

This is working well for me right now. About 90% of my sales are organic, and I know Amazon is sending emails recommending my books to readers every day.

CREATING Amazon ads that convert

Just like Facebook ads and BookBub ads, it's important to make sure your Amazon ads convert as well as getting clicks. In fact, this could be even more important for Amazon ads because conversions are taken into account when the system is deciding whether to serve your ads.

One of the benefits of Amazon ads is that you get free impressions, so people will only pay when they click on your ad. This means you get plenty of eyeballs in front of your book for free. But beware: this can actually damage your success.

If you're getting hundreds or thousands of people

looking at your book, but not clicking on the ad or buying it, Amazon will learn that your book doesn't sell. And over time, it will stop serving your ad.

I've worked hard on my targeting, and I regularly refine the category targets that I use, to make sure I'm only targeting categories that convert. This way Amazon knows that if somebody clicks on one of those ads, they've got a good chance of buying the book. And this in turn means that Amazon is more likely to serve my ads.

Making sure that your Amazon ads convert and doing plenty of testing not only will help you sell more books, but it will help you serve more ads. A virtuous circle!

Paid mailing lists

The fourth option you have for paid advertising is newsletters and mailing lists. This includes lists such as Freebooksy, Robin Reads, Red Feather Romance, and many more. It also includes BookBub featured deals (which are different from BookBub ads).

Let's take a look at how paid mailing lists can drive the three different types of sale.

SELLING books using paid lists

Provided your book is on offer or free, selling books using these newsletters isn't hard. The people on those mailing lists are hungry for deals, and they'll buy a lot of the books that they see. If you get a BookBub featured deal, that can drive thousands of sales in one day.

However, as we'll see in the next section, they're not always the best sales in the long run. I wouldn't advise using these newsletters early on in your author career or in the life of an individual book. Let's see why.

Using paid lists to sell books to the right people.
This is where I think paid mailing lists fall down.

The targeting is very poor or sometimes non-existent. You'll be targeting readers of a very broad genre, and what's more those readers will be unlikely to buy at full price: not good for a sustainable career.

If I'd used paid newsletters early on to sell my books, I would have been giving Amazon poor data. And I didn't think getting more short-term sales was worth that.

This was a mistake I made with my earlier books (during my wilderness years of selling barely anything). I ran deals to the newsletters (including BookBub featured deals), and I saw my also-boughts suffer. Instead of my also-boughts being similar books to mine, they were other books that featured in the same newsletter on the same day. This was the worst when I got a BookBub featured deal – the existing data wasn't strong enough, so just one day of data wiped it out.

Paid newsletters can have also an adverse effect on reviews. People outside your target audience will be buying the book and might not enjoy it as much as your target audience. Only you can judge whether you're happy to take that hit.

I wouldn't advise using paid newsletters until you've established a baseline level of sales, and you know that Amazon is recommending your book to the right people and getting you organic sales.

Once you're at that stage, you'll find that the data blip

on the day of the deal doesn't cause too many problems, and it's quickly overridden in the following days and weeks.

Using paid lists to drive conversions

Conversion rates aren't an issue with paid lists. As long as your book's on offer or free, you'll find that you'll get hundreds or thousands of sales or downloads.

If you want lots of sales and conversions, and you know your existing data on also-boughts is solid, they can be a good way to temporarily boost sales and get your book more visibility.

* * *

And there it is: this is how I use different advertising platforms to sell my books. When I started out, I was focused not just on volume of sales, but on the quality of those sales and the data that they provided to Amazon.

If you're going to be a full-time author and write best-selling books, you need to ensure Amazon knows who to recommend your book to, so can sow the seeds for a long-term career with minimum effort. Each ad platform will help you do this in a different way.

25

ADAPTING FOR FUTURE RELEASES

The more books you write and launch, the easier it will get, and the less attention you'll have to pay to each launch.

Personally, I don't do a lot of marketing for each new book launch.

I'll send two or three emails to my newsletter, write a couple of Facebook posts (often including a video at the 'crime scene'), post one or two tweets and add the book to my Amazon ads – and that's pretty much it. I don't run Facebook ads to books that aren't the first in series because I know that enough of my fans will buy the book and I want new readers to start at the beginning. But you might consider running ads in the launch period, maybe in the first month. After that, profitability is likely to drop.

If I'm releasing the first book in a new series, that'll look very different, because I want that to reach a new audience and not just my existing readers. I'll run (and test) Facebook ads to the new book, promote it using social media, and maybe run a blog tour. I'll wait until the first book is selling and the second book is on pre-order and then I'll start running Amazon ads on a low budget. My marketing plan will look very similar to what I did for my first series, as detailed in the previous chapter.

How do you adapt your launch strategy to subsequent books in a series or later books in your career?

The key thing is to take note of what you did for your first book, what worked and what didn't. Repeat what works and review what didn't. How could you improve on it? Do you need to drop it?

You might find that some methods start working once you have a bigger backlist, even if they didn't work for your first book. Test everything – but don't forget to spend most of your time writing the next book.

The biggest bonus once you have multiple books out is that read-through will boost the value of a sale of one book. If 1,000 people buy and read one of your books, and then 500 of them go on to buy another, then your first sale is worth 50% more. This means you can increase your ad budget and afford more expensive clicks. If you write in series, you'll maximise the chances of this. And if you don't, it pays to write books in the same genre and make sure your cover branding is tight.

There are a few ways you can help this along. Include a link to the next book in your back matter, with a paragraph or blurb encouraging readers to buy it. Put the next book on preorder, so people have something to click on as soon as they've finished the current one. And use your newsletter to remind fans of all your books, not just the ones they've read.

BUT THE MOST reliable way to keep selling more books with each one you write is to write great books that readers love. If you've done your research and you understand your market, then your readers will be crying out for more. With each release, you'll have to spend less time and money on marketing, and you can spend more time on writing. Bonus!

IN THE NEXT section of this book, I'm going to move on to look at how you build a sustainable author career. I'll include ways you can build a loyal following and ensure you continue enjoying it without suffering from burnout. After all, you got into this because you love it, right?

26

LAUNCH RESOURCES

Here are some of the resources on launching that have been helpful for me.

Books

- *Launch to Market* by Chris Fox
- *Relaunch Your Novel* by Chris Fox
- *Amazon Ads Unleashed* by Robert J Ryan
- *Sales Copy Unleashed* by Robert J Ryan
- *Writing Killer Cover Copy* by Elana Johnson
- *Amazon Decoded* by David Gaughran
- *BookBub Ads* by David Gaughran

Courses

- Ads for Authors by Mark Dawson
- Self Publishing 101 by Mark Dawson
- Starting from Zero by David Gaughran

Podcasts

- The Self Publishing Show
- The Creative Penn
- Six-figure Authors

PART V

STEP FIVE - LONGEVITY

27

THE TWO FACES OF A SUSTAINABLE AUTHOR CAREER

If you're going to make a go of being a professional author in the long term, there are two things that you need to get right.

The first one is readers.

You'll need to build an army of superfans who come back and buy your books again and again. This way, you'll know you've got a guaranteed level of sales with each new release. And you can spend your time writing instead of marketing and trying to find new readers.

The second is *you*.

Even if you're successful in selling hundreds of thousands of books, if you don't enjoy it, what's the point? You might as well go back and get a day job with a pension and healthcare and everything else that comes with it.

IN THIS PART of the book, we'll look at how you can build a long-term career both by generating loyalty amongst your fans, and by ensuring that it works for you over the years, and you continue to enjoy it.

28

BUILD AN ARMY OF FANS

To become a bestselling author and sustain a long-term career, you need fans.

If you have to go out and sell every new book to a new audience, then you'll quickly burn out. You'll spend so much time marketing you won't be able to enjoy the writing.

But if you can build an army of superfans, then not only will it help you sell books, it will also be immensely satisfying.

I love getting feedback from my fans. I love the fact that people recommend my books to their friends, and that they talk about my characters as if they're real. It's one of the most satisfying and enjoyable things about being an author.

Let's take a look at some of the techniques you can use to nurture your fans and make sure they're with you for the long haul.

Your reader newsletter

Earlier in this book, I talked about paid newsletters as a form of advertising. I didn't talk about your own newsletter or mailing list.

If you don't already have one of these, then you need to create one right now. Go on. Right. Now. This book will still be here when you've done it. I can wait. It's never too early to set up your newsletter, and it's never too late, either.

Your reader newsletter is the single most effective way of maintaining a long-term relationship with your fans.

You may already have a great social media presence. But what if Facebook suddenly disappears? What if Twitter blocks you?

Social media is fickle. It changes from year to year and if you want a career that spans decades, the most reliable way to keep in touch with your readers is via email.

I know some people will tell you that email is dead, and it's an old-fashioned form of marketing. But the reality is that it's the only way of engaging with your readers that you have full control over. (And if email were dead and old-fashioned, I doubt Amazon would invest so much effort into curating and emailing you their recommendations every day.)

OK, so you'll use a mailing list provider. But the data that's collected for you (i.e. the email addresses of your readers) is yours. If your mailing list provider goes bust, you can download that data and migrate it to another mailing list provider.

If Facebook goes bust there's no way you can move the names of all your followers to Instagram or Twitter. (For starters, Instagram would have gone bust too because it's owned by Facebook.)

The other benefit is that you have more control over how many of your readers see your emails. I know that email deliverability can be a challenge, and emails can bypass people's inboxes – but there are things you can do to make sure more of your emails get past spam filters. You have more control over these than you do over posts that you add to social media, which can be shown or not shown to your followers at the whim of that day's algorithm.

I'm not saying don't do social media. If you enjoy using social media and there are channels where your readers hang out, then by all means make use of them. But encourage those fans to join your mailing list, too.

The best way to encourage people to join your mailing list is to have a reader magnet: a free story, novella or even full-length book that people get when they first join the list. When I first started offering a novella, signups to my newsletter shot up. People appreciate the fact that I've given them a book for free.

If you don't have an email list yet, write yourself a reader magnet, set up a newsletter and start using it to communicate with your readers.

I won't go into detail here as to what you should write in your newsletter or how often you should send it. But what I can say is that it's definitely worth doing.

Don't disappoint your readers

Your readers will have come to you because you write a certain kind of book. They'll know you for the genre(s) that you write in and the style of your writing.

They'll also get used to your publishing schedule. If you're with a publishing house, this will be set by them. If you're indie, you have control over this – but it's worth building a regular schedule and sticking to it so your readers know what to expect.

If you decide to switch genres, you might find that you lose a lot of readers. Many authors who do this prefer to use a new pen name, so they don't dilute their readership. That can work well, but it does mean twice as much work. If you've got two pen names, that means two mailing lists, two websites and two social media presences. You might choose not to do all that, but it's worth bearing in mind.

Alternatively, don't even think about changing genres. Stick with the genre you're writing. Try different approaches to it, but stay within the same broad frame.

For example, I write crime (as you might have noticed). My first series was a gritty police procedural set in Birmingham. I deliberately made Birmingham feel like another character. The books have an urban feel to them. A lot of the action takes place at night, often in the more down-at-heel parts of the city. My second series, while still a police procedural, is set in Dorset. I focus on atmospheric and windswept locations rather than idyllic ones. But even so, the tone is slightly different because of the location. It also means I get to write about fields, hills and beaches, instead of industrial estates and litter-strewn canals. I enjoy the variety that gives me, but by writing in the same genre I'm not disappointing my readers. It certainly doesn't hurt that there are crossover characters between the two series, too.

There are ways you can continue to keep your readers happy over the long term without having to write the same books time and again, or the same characters time and again.

Engage with your readers

When your readers get in touch with you and give you feedback, you should celebrate. Take the time to reply and thank them.

I respond to every reader email, even though this now takes me more time than I spend writing.

Sometimes, it's tempting to ignore those emails and not engage – after all, I've got words to write. But I remind myself that without those readers, I wouldn't have a career. I wouldn't be able to spend my time writing and would have to go back to my day job.

I also thank my readers for reviews. I don't do it directly: I never respond to reviews themselves. But when my books reach a certain number of reviews, I will post to Facebook or I'll write a newsletter, thanking people for those reviews and telling them how much difference it makes to me.

Then there'll be readers who get in touch with corrections. They'll spot a typo or a continuity error in a book. It's not criticism: it's help. Some of my readers are so good at spotting errors, I've invited them to join my beta team. They love that they can play a part in polishing the books.

It's also worth giving your biggest fans extra attention. I could name the people who are the most highly engaged with my books. They regularly message me on Facebook, tweet to me, write blog posts about my books, or send me emails. I make sure that when I reply to them, I do so in a way that makes it clear that I know who they are, and that way there's an ongoing communication. I don't treat them the same was I'd treat somebody who's contacted me for the first time.

These readers are your superfans: the lifeblood of your author business. Nurture them, and you'll have a career.

29

WIBBOW AND KNOWING YOUR PRIORITIES

The acronym WIBBOW stands for 'Would I be better off writing?'

Once you become a full-time author, the days will suddenly stretch out in front of you. You'll feel like you have too much time on your hands because you haven't got a day job to worry about.

What should you be filling that time with?

Well, my answer is writing.

No matter how effective any marketing tactic, the best thing you can be doing to nurture your long-term career is to write the next book. Written ten books? An eleventh will add 10% to your revenue (probably more). Written twenty? A twenty-first will still add revenue, and might get the attention of people who haven't read the others. Just think, they can now buy 21 books from you.

Now I'm not saying you don't need to do any marketing or business at all. These things are essential. But they should account for a minority of your time.

When a new idea comes to you, or a fan or fellow

author suggests something that you think might be fun or help you sell books, ask yourself: 'Would I be better off writing? Would I sell more books and keep my readers happy by doing this, or by writing?'

WIBBOW IS PARTICULARLY useful for some of the activities that might seem pressing or fun, but aren't proven ways to sell books in big numbers. Things like:

- author signings (with travel, how much time are you giving up for how many sales?)
- book readings (people will be no more likely to buy the book after hearing you read from it, sorry)
- interviews and podcasts (only useful if the audience is your target market)
- tweaking your website (you can get lost down this rabbit hole)
- Facebook launch parties or online 'ask me anything' sessions (they'll attract the people who buy your books anyway)
- meetings with agents or publishers to discuss things that could be agreed over the phone or by email.

ALL OF THESE things might have a place, if they'll help you nurture your fans (some authors host very successful online launch parties). But if you're not sure, ask yourself: 'WIBBOW?' If the answer is yes, you can say no to the activity.

• • •

There's another time when you can throw WIBBOW out of the window: if you love doing the activity that's on offer. I know writers who'll engage in marketing activities that aren't particularly effective at selling books, and could be seen as a waste of time, but that they love. Sometimes I do it myself. Life's too short not to enjoy yourself: but beware spending too much time on fun, as you do have books to write.

(*Important note: chatting to people on social media does not come under this heading, it's a time suck.*)

And if you're worried about saying no to people?

You have the perfect excuse.

In my experience, no one has ever pushed back when I've told them 'I'm so sorry I can't do x, but I have a book deadline.' People respect the need for a writer to write. And they'll be impressed by your professionalism.

Make sure you only do things that create more stories for your readers to enjoy, that sell books, or that you love doing.

30

WHEN TO GET HELP

I've already talked about the fact that you'll need to involve professionals in your writing career.

If you're traditionally published, those professionals will be your agent (if you have one), and the people at your publishing house.

If you're an indie, you'll need to hire an editor, proofreader and cover designer, maybe someone to format your book or to help you market it.

But over time, your needs will change. The more books you sell, the busier you'll become. You'll have more demands on your time, a bigger inbox to clear every day and more data to analyse. And you'll get more attention.

How do you manage all this while still getting those words down and producing books?

The answer is to hire help.

Some authors set up their own company and take on employees. I've employed my son to help me with data analysis and publishing.

But it's more common to hire freelancers to help with

specific tasks. You're already using editors, proof-readers and cover designers as freelancers but there are more people you can work with.

You might hire a virtual assistant to take the more mundane admin off you. You might hire an expert on data and spreadsheets to monitor your marketing campaigns. You might hire somebody to manage your marketing for you or to run ads and monitor them.

It can be hard to let go of these tasks, particularly if you're an indie and you've enjoyed setting up and establishing your writing business.

But as you become busier and as your time becomes more precious, the important thing to identify is which parts of your business only you can work on.

The core part of that is the writing. Only you can write your books.

(Note: some authors work with co-writers or ghost writers to reduce the writing workload, but it's rare.)

For most authors, the writing will be the thing that you need to keep doing. You'll need to find ways to free up your time so that you can keep writing without burning out.

You might choose to hire a family member or bring your partner into the business. You might work formally with another author and reduce duplication of effort. Or you might hire a business manager to take care of the business side of things.

Whichever way you do this will have to be suited to your own circumstances: the way you work, the aspects of the business that you enjoy and are good at, and what you feel comfortable delegating.

I know I find it difficult to let go. I've recently hired a

virtual assistant and I'm slowly passing over responsibility for tasks. These are things I don't need to be doing myself, but that I'm used to doing, and it feels odd to let go. But I know that if I do that, it means more time for writing books and engaging with my readers.

If you can try and think creatively about bringing other people into your business, you can find ways to create more books or free up more time – and to avoid burnout through overwork.

31

OWNING YOUR WORK

As you develop your career, it pays to understand intellectual property and copyright, so that you can make the most of your work in the long term.

Thinking this way isn't necessarily going to help you become a bestselling author, but it will help you maintain a long-term career and protect your earnings over time.

Depending on where you live, the specifics will differ. But in most countries, copyright belongs to the person who creates a piece of work – unless they sign it over to somebody else. It's rare for copyright to change hands for novels, but it can happen for nonfiction.

If you sign over copyright to your work, it's no longer yours. It belongs to the publisher. If you want control over your work and your career, I'd advise retaining that copyright. A good publisher won't expect you to hand over copyright. What they *will* want is to be assigned or licensed specific publishing rights. Which are the rights to publish and distribute your work, either across the board, or in specific formats, languages or territories.

. . .

I'M NEITHER a lawyer nor an expert on copyright and intellectual property, but I have taken time to research them and learn how they apply to my home country, which is the UK.

I've done this so that when I'm talking to publishers or other people that want to license rights to my work, I know what I'm talking about.

I WON'T GO into detail about IP and rights here. And this is NOT legal advice (don't sue me, please). But I would advise getting your head around a few key points:

- If you sell rights to a book, it doesn't have to be in all formats, languages and/or territories. It can be split up.
- If a publisher isn't going to make use of rights in a certain format, language or territory, then it makes sense for you to retain those rights, so you can sell them elsewhere or make use of them yourself. Ask if they'll use all the rights.
- Try not to license rights for the term of copyright. In the UK, this lasts until 70 years after you die. I know I want my kids (and grandkids) to benefit from that, not a publisher who's unlikely to be marketing my books by then.
- Some contracts will include rights for formats not yet invented. Personally I'd never sign a contract with this clause in it, as I don't want to sell something when I don't even know what it is.

- Splitting up rights will normally be better for you financially, as you're selling more things to more people.
- Read all of your contracts yourself. All the way through. Don't rely on someone else (not even your agent). And don't assume that because a contract or clause is 'boilerplate' or 'standard', that you can't negotiate.

UNDERSTANDING IP IS useful if you're seeking a publishing contract or if you're hybrid. And for long-standing indies, going hybrid becomes almost an inevitability, especially when it comes to translations and audio. TV and film too, if you're lucky.

Take the time to understand what those clauses mean and don't be afraid to ask why a clause is in there. I've asked dumb questions in contract negotiations and never regretted it.

32

ADAPTING TO CHANGE

If you're going to have a long-term author career, then the chances are that the publishing landscape will change many times over the course of that career. And that's why it's important not to tie yourself to any particular method you use to write or to sell books.

I've tried to keep this book as high level and strategic as I can. I know that in one or two of the chapters (the chapter on seeding sales, for example), I've been more detailed and tactical and examined some of the options available to you right now. But the reality is that if you can focus on the high-level priorities and goals and adjust the detail as you go along, then you're much more likely to be successful.

It's vital that you write great books that readers love to read: that will never change.

It's vital that you nurture your army of fans, and that you engage with them. That too will never change.

It's also vital that you bring in new readers and

encourage a new audience to find your work. What will change is the method that you use to do that.

Let's look at some specific examples of things that can throw a loop for your author career.

Changes to what marketing methods work

Just because a marketing tactic was working for you last year, that doesn't mean it will work again this year.

Maybe the cost per click on Amazon ads has become too high. Maybe there's an election on and it's pushing up the price of Facebook ads. Maybe the paid newsletters you used to rely on have dropped your genre.

You'll need to monitor the effectiveness of your tactics: things like publishing channels, pricing, advertising, and social media. Track what works and what stops working, and make changes. Test new ideas and new techniques.

Keep your eye on what's going on in the publishing industry, and what new technologies and ideas are coming up. Learn from the experts who are at the forefront of any changes. Listening to podcasts and reading the trade press will help as well as attending conferences and being engaged in author networks. Always remembering, of course, to ask yourself the golden question: WIBBOW?

If you can be flexible and nimble, and not weld yourself to tactics, then you can sustain a long-term career and carry on writing for decades.

If you lose your publishing contract

If you're traditionally published, the biggest upheaval is if your publisher doesn't commission your next book.

This means you'll need to make a choice. Are you going

to stop writing, publish the next book independently, or seek a new publisher?

Which one of those is right for you will depend on your individual circumstances. But it's a huge upheaval, and something it's worth being prepared for.

Authors have very little security in their publishing contracts with their publishers. If your publisher is taken over, the chances are you'll have less security than the publisher's employees. They can drop you between books or at the end of your multi-book contract. Unless there are specific provisions to the contrary in your contract, there's nothing to stop them.

Keep your eye on what other publishers are doing – and what indie publishers are doing as well so that you have options if the worst should happen.

If (when!) the market shifts

I've talked a lot in this book about understanding your genre: the market for books in it and the popular tropes. But these change over time. Sometimes quickly, sometimes over long time periods.

From time to time, a new subgenre will suddenly appear. Some nimble indies will probably jump in and grab that territory. But if you've got your eye on your genre, you might be able to carve out a little space in it for yourself.

Or you might decide not to follow the short-term trends and stick with your long-term strategy. Even if you do that, the trends within your genre could change. So, for example, in my genre of crime, what's popular right now certainly wasn't popular twenty years ago. The authors who've adapted their style are the ones with long-term careers.

Keep reading. Don't just read your favourite authors:

read new books, the books that are getting people's attention, the ones climbing to the top of the charts.

Don't copy them. But be aware of them, in case you need to adapt your own style to suit the market.

If your personal circumstances change

Maybe you're happy with your publishing schedule. You're writing four books a year, managing your business effectively, tweaking your marketing as things changes and doing nicely.

But then disaster hits. You become sick. You get pregnant (maybe not a disaster!). A family member is sick. Or perhaps an injury means you can't sit at a desk and write.

It's almost impossible to anticipate and prepare for things like this. But what you can do is give yourself an insurance policy in the form of savings.

I keep two business savings accounts. One has the money I'll need to pay my taxes at the end of the year (don't forget to set that money aside). The other contains the equivalent of a year's salary in my last day job, adjusted for inflation. That's my insurance. I know that if something happened to me, I'd be able to carry on paying the bills for a year. Hopefully that would give me the time to get things back on track.

You might have an alternative backup. A day job. Investments. Property. A partner earning a regular salary. Whatever it is, it can give you peace of mind. It won't help with the upheaval of the disastrous life event, but it will mean you can still put food on the table.

* * *

THOSE ARE JUST four example of changes that could impact your career, if you're not ready for them. If you're prepared and have backup plans, then you'll recover more quickly. And you won't be playing catchup and trying to recap lost sales or start again from scratch.

33

LOVING WHAT YOU DO AND AVOIDING BURNOUT

Being an author can be stressful.

There's uncertainty about how well the next book will land. Will your readers be disappointed by it and refuse to buy it? Will your publisher drop you after the end of this series? Well the reviewers slate your next book and your reputation go down the tube?

Even as a bestseller it's common to worry about your career dipping. And there's also the stress of deadlines. You always have a deadline ahead of you. It might be the first draft or edits, proofreading, publication or a marketing campaign. The deadlines keep coming thick and fast. And they always seem to loom up when you least need them to.

If you're writing fast, the pressure of hitting your word count every day can become a headache. Sometimes it all feels so hard. Why did you become an author, again?

So, how do you maintain a long-term author career without all this stress and uncertainty causing you burnout?

For me, the answer is to make sure that I keep doing work that I love.

That means writing books that inspire me creatively and challenge me intellectually, as well as being fun to write.

I tend to start a new series every year. I'm somebody who struggles doing the same thing year in, year out. Back in the days when I had a regular job, I used to change jobs every two years.

Nowadays, my equivalent is to change characters and locations. Once a series is established, I'm already planning the next one.

I may still have a few books to write in the current series, or I may overlap them. But I'm always thinking about what comes next. I enjoy being able to travel to different locations for research and having different characters in my head each year. For me, writing about the same characters in the same places for the rest of my writing life would be just as dull as a day job.

WHAT STIMULATES you will be different. The important thing is to identify what you love about your writing. If you discover that what you're currently doing is no longer what you love, there's no harm in taking a break and reassessing.

You could start again in a different genre, using the skills that you've developed to become a success already. Plenty of authors have done it.

It's worth keeping some financial backup for this (see the previous chapter). That way, you have time to start over in your new genre without financial pressure.

. . .

IF YOU'RE FINDING that the pace of your writing is causing you stress and making it unenjoyable, then you can always slow down. If you've got a solid backlist behind you, that'll make you an income and there's no reason you can't write fewer books each year.

I know that's something I'm going to be doing in the next couple of years. I've been hustling for the last few years, scrambling to get myself established in my genre and writing quickly in order to do so. But I know that I can't keep writing as fast as I am and still have the time to enjoy life.

KEEP an eye on your mental health. Check in with yourself from time to time to make sure you're still enjoying it. If not, try to find ways to make the writing more fun. Or take a break, or slow down.

After all, we became writers because we loved it. If we'd been happy earning money in a job that we hated, we'd go back to the regular job with the pension and the health insurance and the rest.

34

LONGEVITY RESOURCES

Here are some of the resources on launching that have been helpful for me.

Books

- *Strangers to Superfans* by David Gaughran
- *Newsletter Ninja* by Tammi LaBrecque

Facebook Groups / Communities

- SPF Community
- 20 Books to 50k

Organisations

- Alliance of Independent Authors
- Society of Authors

BECOMING A BESTSELLER

Thank you for reading this book. I hope you've found it helpful and that it's given you some ideas, tips or inspiration.

I know it's hard to make a living as an author. It's even harder to become a bestseller. But I don't think it's impossible – in fact I know it's not impossible – and I know there isn't some magic fairy dust you need to sprinkle over yourself to get there.

Instead, I think it's all about hard work, insight, and the right attitude. That's what I've used to become a bestseller myself, and I hope it works for you too.

Here's a recap of the five steps to becoming a successful author.

Mindset

- Start thinking like a pro. None of the other steps will work without the right mindset.

- When someone asks you what you do, tell them, 'I'm a writer'. Own it.
- Surround yourself with people who think like professionals and take inspiration from them.
- Make writing a habit - show up every day. Writers write.
- Banish the myth of writer's block - don't worry about how good it is, just get the words down.

Research

It's essential to understand your market, your genre, and how to write stories that readers love.

- Your genre – the niches and the tropes. What do readers expect?
- The market – your comps, what's new, which books are rising and which are falling in the charts. Know where your book fits.
- Story and craft – what resonates with readers. Read lots, and take note of what works. Read craft books to learn how to write compelling stories.

Craft

You'll never be a bestseller if you don't write well. Take the time to refine your craft and become a better writer with each book.

- Identify the sweet spot between what you love, what readers love, and what you're good at.

- Take time to understand what aspects of story readers love - it might not be what you think.
- Write lots – it's the best way to become a better writer. Forget any snobbery about prolific writers being hacks - it's a myth.

Launch

Now it's time to put your book or series out into the world. Make sure it's ready and you know where to target it.

- Research routes to market for your genre and decide which will work for you.
- Get your book into the best shape you can - editing, proofreading, beta readers.
- Professional packaging – cover and blurb must sell the book.
- Test advertising and other methods to seed sales and start finding readers.

Longevity

The biggest challenge can be maintaining a long-term author career once you've achieved success.

- Nurture your fans – they are the life blood of your career.
- Keep learning and adapting – what works now might not in the future.
- Make sure you love it – if you don't, you might as well find a regular job.

* * *

IF YOU CAN FORGE a long-term career writing books that you love writing and readers love reading, then you've hit the jackpot. I hope that this book has given you inspiration on how to do it, and that it helps you achieve success.

Happy writing!

ACKNOWLEDGMENTS

I've now written so many novels that I no longer leave acknowledgments in the end of my books.

It's something I did in my first book, because it felt grand and authorial. But this book is different, because there are people who have helped me get to the point where I am today, selling thousands of books, and confident enough to pass on my knowledge to help others do the same.

* * *

In 2003, I attended a business writing course run by Rob Ashton of Emphasis Training. During that course, we had to mind-map a project we were working on. I didn't actually have any business writing projects running at the time, so I started mind mapping a novel instead. That novel became my first book, but wasn't published for many years. It doesn't sell all that well (not Rob's fault), but without that workshop, and that novel, I never would have started.

Birmingham Writers' Group got me writing when I really needed a kick up the arse. I've been an active member for many years now and it's thanks to them that I never stop writing. The feedback they've given me on my manuscripts has been invaluable, as well as the support and encouragement. Thanks in particular to Martin Sullivan, Hazel Ward,

Chris Garghan, Kirsty Handley, Julie Spicer, Simon Fairbanks, Berni Sorga-Millwood and David Croser-Drake.

Heide Goody and Iain Grant are two ultra-talented indie authors who inspired me to publish my own books. I'd been hawking my manuscript around agents for a while, and still wasn't entirely convinced that it was the right route for me. But I didn't believe that self-publishing was viable. Heide and Iain showed me otherwise. They'd been writing and publishing books and building an audience for a number of years. And watching them do it – and enjoy it at the same time – made me believe that I could make a success of it too.

John Bowen gave me the confidence to believe that you could successfully market books. I met John at an author networking event in Birmingham and it quickly became clear that he knew a hell of a lot more than I did about marketing. So I picked his brains. When I started marketing my crime books, deep in lockdown, he and I had long chats and video calls, in which he gave me advice and feedback on my ads. He constantly encouraged me while I was running those preorder ads, despite the fact that it felt very risky. And having him as a cheerleader really boosted my confidence.

Joel Hames is my editor, and the person most closely involved in my writing business. I knew him as a writer before we started working together formally. He writes crime and thrillers but with a more literary bent than me. It makes him the perfect editor because he's a great writer. And he also understands the genre. He knows when I'm writing in a certain way in order to appeal to readers, and he knows what else is selling and what the trends are. Joel has made my writing better than it was, and he's helped me target my writing towards my market. I know he'll be editing these acknowledgments and I hope he's not too embarrassed by this.

I have a fantastic network of writer friends who provide advice, encouragement, and laughs. They understand the frustrations of writing and selling books. And many of them helped fact-check this book. Thanks to Justin Anderson, RE Vance, Judi Daykin, Christie Adams, David Milnes, Kim Nash, Michele Pariza Wacek, Mary Kingswood, JD Kirk, Tao Wong and Daisy James.

My dad was the very first person to read my first book. As all good dads do, he told me it was wonderful (it really wasn't). Now he's part of my beta reading team. He's particularly good at spotting continuity errors and anything to do with gardening or the seasons, because he's an allotmenteer. The encouragement he's given me and the fact that he has pressed my books into the hands of family and friends have been a real boost, particularly at times when I wasn't selling well.

Without my readers I'd have no author career. Some of them have been immensely loyal to my books and characters, and have even become beta readers and helped forge the books. Thanks to Nicola Southall, Dave Barden, Claire Baker, Anne Andreas and Nigel Adams – and everyone else, too many of you to mention. Also to Fiona Twycross and Claire Jenkins, longstanding friends who've shared my books far and wide.

I'd also like to credit the publishing experts whose work I've learned from and used extensively in developing my own career. I apologise if I've pinched any of their ideas in this book.

Those people include, but aren't limited to: Joanna Penn, Mark Dawson, David Gaughran, Orna Ross, Debbie Young, Sacha Black, Chris Fox, Mark Stay, Mark Desvaux, Kristine Kathryn Rusch, Dean Wesley Smith, Robert J. Ryan, Tammi Labrecque and Elana Johnson. I've listed their books or resources in the relevant parts of this book. If their name is on this list, it's because I think they're worth listening to!

I'm hugely grateful to them for sharing their expertise and making it so much easier for the rest of us to follow on behind them. Long may it continue.

Printed in Great Britain
by Amazon